Within Each of Us

To Riley

Merry Christmas
& Joy

Klaus

Within Each of Us

A Journey of Awakening
to Inner Guidance

Dino Calabrese

River Sanctuary
PUBLISHING

Within Each of Us: A Journey of Awakening to Inner Guidance
Copyright © 2011 by Dino Calabrese

Cover painting by Dino Calabrese

Cover design by Markos-Cory Moreno
Interior design by DreamWriter (Dreamwriterservices.com)

ISBN 978-1-935914-05-1

Printed in the United States of America

RIVER SANCTUARY PUBLISHING
P.O Box 1561
Felton, CA 95018
www.riversanctuarypublishing.com
Dedicated to the spiritual awakening of the New Earth

*To my nieces
Alexandra and Victoria
and my nephew Steven*

Contents

~ 1 ~

My Early Years

The faith that we possess through intuition is the Mind of God within us forever proclaiming its own being. We may trust its inspiration; it is nothing less than the proclamation of the infinite in our own soul.

Ernest Holmes

When you plug an electrical cord into a power outlet, you get connected. If you get connected to an electrical plant, you can charge and light up an entire state. When your energy hooks up to another source of energy, you get charged up. When your energy gets connected to the ultimate energy source, you can light up the world. I think this is what you call total love. Unconditional love. This is God.

I am a designer, and I am also an intuitive. I interpret vibrations.

People always ask, "When did you realize that you had special powers, or the ability to use your intuition?" It is hard to know how to answer that question – how does one explain? We all have the ability; we just have to figure it out. But how? Every one of us has had the experience of hearing voices in our mind that seem to communicate from some "other place." We also seem to know – that is, have a certain feeling – when that voice is saying something worth listening to. When you hear voices in your mind that *feel*

1

correct to you, could these communications be from beings from some other (nonphysical) world attempting to speak to you? How many of us, having shared these feelings with others, were told that our brain is playing tricks on us? We may even have been told that we're crazy!

The Mystery of Childhood

My childhood was a mysterious time for me. As a young child, I could never understand why, when my parents would have a conversation, they seemed to always argue. When they argued, my heart would hurt. I would constantly get ear infections.

Looking back on this experience later, I couldn't help but wonder if my body was reacting to this energy. Did being around their negative energy make my heart hurt? Were the ear infections my body's way of telling me that I no longer wanted to hear the arguing? Instead of shutting down all together and going deaf, my ears would get inflamed with pain from infection.

I remember being hospitalized when I was very young. I sat in a hospital bed all alone for what seemed to be an eternity. As an adult, I found papers in my parents' belongings which stated that I was admitted for anorexia. How could a child of four feel that bad about himself that his body would close down?

Hearing music always made my body feel so good and free, flowing with the vibration of each note. Instead of questioning, I just trusted that this was good for my soul, because it felt like the right thing for me to do. It seemed my cells were in harmony when I heard music. I escaped from my parents' reality to my own. It was as if I was drawn to something that lived deep in my soul.

I never liked playing with other children. Was it because

I was raised on my parents' planet? Or was it that I did not feel a connection playing with other children? For some reason, I never felt lonely when playing by myself. There always seemed to be someone next to me. At the time, I didn't even consider whether that was an imaginary friend or a Spirit who wanted to keep me company. It didn't really matter, because I just knew I never felt alone.

I would find out years later what it truly meant. When playing with other children, there always seemed to be a point at which I had to conform to what they wanted. If I did not, it ended up with someone either taking something away from me, or hitting me, or some other negative outcome. That would always leave me sad or empty.

I suppose it would have been easier to play the way others wanted me to play. It just did not seem right to me. Why was it a problem when I played in the way that felt natural to me? When I was growing up in the 1960's, all boys played a certain way that was very different from little girls. That was very difficult for me, because when I did try to play like the others, it just did not feel I was being true to myself. I felt like there was a big empty hurt inside my stomach – or in my entire *being*. I just could never feel complete and whole inside when I did not follow what felt good.

And yet I kept trying to interact with other children the way I was told to do it. The more I tried, the more I would either screw up, or not feel good about what I was doing. It was never enough to just enjoy the trees and the birds. Never enough to just be able to dance or to draw what you wanted to draw. There was no other alternative but to be like all the other little boys.

God forbid you should be like the little girls.... If you wanted to enjoy seeing the world like a little girl, you surely had to be totally homosexual, which of course turned out to be the most serious taboo in life. I did like to play trucks and build forts, but that seemed to not matter. Drawing, dancing, and liking music instead of fighting and playing sports was just believed to be wrong. So how in the world could a boy be creative? I wondered. Was Picasso thought to be a sissy until he had sex with many women – and only then he was considered to be an artist?

My Secret Friend

The only thing I became sure of in those early years of my life was that when I did what felt right to me, happiness always surrounded me. The old Joy bug. When I tried, and believe me I tried, to be other than what was resonating in my heart, I just wanted to hide in a hole and die.

In school, I tried to understand what the teachers were teaching. I truly did. It just did not compute. I felt really bad. I just could not comprehend what they were trying to tell me. When I studied art and music, that felt good to me, and I got it. It was very joyous. My parents did not support me when I wanted to pursue anything that had to do with art or music. I knew from the time I was five years old that I was an artist. That is where my passion always was and where my heart felt the best. Five, which is the earliest I can remember. Before that, life was kind of a blur to me.

Five years my senior, my older brother had very little to do with me. Years later, in my twenties, I was told by a psychic that my mother had a miscarriage before I was born. He had asked me if, in my childhood, I had felt like I had someone with me who played with me and kept me company. I told him all I knew was that when I was alone, I never felt alone. When I was around other people, I felt alone. I told him that I had no knowledge of my mother losing a child.

That evening I went home and asked my mother if she lost a child before I was born. She was dumb-struck and wanted to know how I found out about this. I told her that I had gone for a reading and this is what the psychic told me. She then shared what no one knew except a few relatives and my father. She had been gaining weight, and the doctor had put her on diet pills. She didn't lose any weight, until about a month later when she went to the bathroom and passed a little baby into the toilet. She had had no idea that she was pregnant. Being Catholic, she felt guilty about it and never wanted anyone to know what had happened.

That was my first confirmation that there were people who could connect to something beyond explanation. At that moment, I acknowledged and welcomed my little friend into my reality. It would be another 30 years, during a conversation with a friend with whom I had grown up, that I would receive more validation. While talking about our childhood, she asked me if I was still in touch with my little friend who would play with me up in the attic. I had no idea what she was talking about. She then told me that she and I would talk about my friend who lived in the closets of our attic. My brother would tell her I was crazy. She said she would always defend me to him, stating that she had two little friends growing up, and that I was entitled to have a little friend as well.

Wow! That interchange confirmed my memories of my childhood, as well as the information I had received earlier from the psychic.

Growing Up Catholic

Going to Catholic school as a child was oppressive, but receiving the Sacraments was inexplicable to a child. Catholic children are required to receive their First

Communion when they are in the second grade. To prepare for this, you have to learn the art of lying in order to succeed in Confession. The purpose of Confession is to release all your sins so that you are pure at the time you receive Communion. We were taught that it was necessary to receive Communion (in case you should die), so that you would be able to get into heaven. Now that is a very intense teaching for a six year old!

I remember studying and then rehearsing with the nuns prior to the big day. Sister Ann Ignatius sat at her desk and directed me to get on my knees, while she pretended to be the priest. I seemed to answer all the questions correctly. Then it was time to do the confessional thing, and I just went blank. "Bless me Father for I have sinned. These are my sins...." and then there was silence. Sister asked me what was wrong. I replied "I have no sins." Sister then said, "Everyone has sins." Then I started to get very nervous, and I said," I have no sins." Once again she said in a voice higher than mine, "Everyone has Sins."

Now I suppose that someone in second grade should have been loaded with sins, but all I could think of was, "I am only six years old. I am incapable of committing sin. My parents would kill me if I committed sin." Still that just did not seem to satisfy Sister Ann Ignatius. Finally after some brutal convincing, I was told to make up some sins. And that is exactly what I did. Now worrying that I was going to Hell for lying to the priest, I made up lies. It did not feel good, not at all. For some reason, I was unable to accept any of this because it did not resonate as truth for me. This went on for about a year, and then I decided that enough is enough. When possible, I would skip out on Confession. Finally, in Fifth Grade I stopped going to church and think that was probably the last time I forced myself to participate in those practices that were disharmonious with my soul.

I Dream to Become an Artist

In Fifth Grade, I finally got the nerve to publicly announce that I wanted to be an artist. Miss Conner, was my 5ᵗʰ Grade teacher. It was the first year that everyone in art class had to purchase a box of pastels prior to the beginning of the school year. I thought this was so cool, but had no idea what one did with them. Finally after about six months into the year we got to use them. As soon as I held those pastels in my hand, I knew that pastels would now be a part of my life. I began to draw and to blend colors together. It was amazing, and the result was an A+ and a Star!

I knew that finally I could say I wanted to become an artist and not care what people thought. Never before had I received validation from either my parents or other family members for doing what made me feel good. After all those years of believing that I could not speak of my passion because it was not right to do so, or it was bad to want to pursue those interests, it took just one experience with a key person to let me know that what I was feeling was a good thing.

From that point on, I determined that I would take responsibility for my own happiness, and that art would now be a part of my life. I accepted the truth about myself. From the time I started school, I had been scared to face the fact that art is what makes me feel good. It was in my thoughts morning, noon and night. Even though I did so want this, I was still in fear of it, and was scared to be who I truly was.

Dancing was already my biggest demon. I loved to dance. To this day, I can watch Fred Astaire twirl Eleanor Powell around the huge glowing stage over and over again, feeling the joy with every tap I hear. I can feel the story that is told in every step that is taken. I cannot tell you how I enjoy watching this man use every inch of his being to express how much he loves. It is mind-boggling to me that others do not hear or feel this to the depth that I do.

A truck driver must love being in control of such a big vehicle, traveling across the country alone with his imagination and thoughts. Or a diver going way down, far into the sea and discovering how another species lives.

I allow each and every person to have their own experience of things that touch them deeply. I determined at that early age that I needed to take the thought of ever dancing out of my consciousness. I can now be an artist. This I can do. Miss Conner said I could be a great artist. Leonardo Da Vinci was a great artist. I chose my confirmation name after him. Every Italian loves him; no one thought that he was strange. This will work. I can fake and pretend that when I grow up, I can become a great painter like Da Vinci. That would be acceptable. I believed that no one would reject this idea and I might actually be able to do something that made me feel good.

Free at Last!

During this period of my life, I found that when I was around many adults, I was always able to hear them better than kids my own age. For some reason, I found their energy to be more patient and wiser. It was like I could read their minds easier, and that just felt right. I wanted to communicate with them more than with those my own age. Kids are really not on the same page as adults. You were always told to either play with the other children, or to keep quiet. I was not able to relate to kids my age. So it was only logical I always felt alone. Was I an old soul? Being so young, was it possible to receive messages by interpreting the vibrations of others? It must be abnormal for a child to relate to an adult, or to read what is on their mind. Best I should keep this quiet too!

After attending Catholic school for ten years, I was asked to leave. As in Fifth Grade, again I had another revelation. I had to let them know that I just did not get it! Nor did I get them. It was too difficult to be a good Italian Catholic boy. My mother was now convinced I was going to Hell. I myself was relieved to leave the school. For the last 14 years, I felt I had already served my life in Hell! What was to become of me now?

The following fall I found myself in a public school. There I was surrounded by three times the amount of students. That meant three times more vibrations to try to understand. Actually, I adjusted better to being in a larger school with more students than I thought I would. You are not as noticed when there are 50 students compared to 20 in a classroom. I could actually close down my energy awareness more easily, and just focus on the books and the teachers. My grades improved as well. I was 15 now, and able to choose what energy I wanted to tune into. I was able to open up to certain vibrations, and close off to the vibrations that did not feel right.

Wow, I began to understand that maybe it is about choice. This thought seemed to work. I was able to see that when I focused on the people with whom I wanted to interact, all worked well. If I chose not to deal with certain people, I just did not have to include them in my reality. It started to become easier. After many years of not knowing how to express what I wanted, now I could choose to be with people who made me feel safe. I could say I was an artist, and feel comfortable with that.

Hopes and New Dreams

In my junior year of high school, one of my projects was to design an album cover. I felt very good with the piece I turned in. My art teacher felt differently, and gave it back.

She told me to do it over. I attempted many times to please her, but she would tear it up and kept saying that I just never did, and never would, get it! I would never be an artist, and I should just give up the thought of being one.

I was as torn as my art project. Memories of my childhood came back to haunt me. I gave up my art! I got through high school by just getting through it. The thought of being an artist left me, and I felt lost once again. I thought of many possibilities of what I might want to be. And then there was the almighty question, "What was the lesson that I came to earth to learn? What was my purpose?"

Everyone always said, "You are here for a reason, to learn a lesson." Since all of my life I wanted to be an artist, and now that got shot down, this must be my lesson to learn. So now what lesson would there be? And who was I to become?

Senior year was a big turning point in my life. I had discovered I could choose certain places and people to play with in my life, and I began to practice everything I had learned! For twelve years of my life, I had not enjoyed school, so I decided to sign up for a work program. That meant I only had to be in class for three hours a day instead of the full day. Since my art bubble was now popped, I had to decide what I wanted to do. What job would be a safe job to have? A job where I could be creative, and yet not be labeled as strange?

I had always wanted to design clothing. But, since designing was now out of the question, maybe retail clothing sales? I chose working in a small men's clothing store. There I learned how to clean, stock shelves, and use a cash register. Soon I started drawing a new type of person into my world. Never really having a motive or an agenda when it came to life, it seemed natural just to love and enjoy everyone. I used to fear being around other people and their energy. Now I was drawing to me a new kind of vibration, people who respected my opinion. How strange and wonderful was that? I was using my intuition to get by, and it was working. I loved this new way of living my life.

After graduation, I continued working through the summer. For the first time, I was feeling quite good about myself. I managed to buy myself a new car. I discovered that there was a whole new energy out in the world that I had never been aware of before. I had always vibrated as my parents did. I came alive with the thrill of having many different options. My love affair with life began.

If It Feels Good, Do It!

That summer, for the first time ever, my older brother and I started to hang out together. There is a five years difference in ages, and we never quite got the Wally and Beaver thing down. One thing that we did have in common was our love for music, and a natural ability to dance, which we got from our father. There was a new trend in Clubs and music called Disco. What an exciting thing! A place where one could be surrounded by total creativity. Great clothes, hair, shoes. Wild dancing and a freeing sound. All new and very exciting. For the first time you could grow your hair, wear platform shoes, glittered socks, and not be a hippie or a freak!

I discovered how good it felt to allow my spirit to run free and to be creative. I knew my life would never be the same. It seemed that every creative person was now moving in a direction, "If it feels good, do it!" And that is exactly what I did. Working all day, and partying all night. Dancing, drinking, smoking, anything and everything. And feeling good about myself afterwards! Not only did I discover that if I used my intuition I could do well with work, but I also could understand people better. I almost always knew what they were thinking. This was very strange and weird.

I remember many times just standing next to a person and feeling their body energy. It would be either very tranquil and comfortable, or very crazy and scary. Once at a party I found myself on the floor with this person who I met, just staring in her eyes by candlelight. All the time feeling so much joy, and I just knew that I would be friends with this person for the rest of my life. (Through many highs and lows, and many different experiences, we have remained good friends to this day.)

I began telling people about their lives and what would be happening to them in the future. More and more people would ask me to give them information. Instead of recognizing that there may be something special in me, I started to feel, once again, different. I did not like the feeling. I wanted to belong and be like everyone else. I stopped giving them messages.

~ 2 ~

Opening to Life

Never limit your view of life by past experience.

Ernest Holmes

Becoming an adult was so much fun and much growth for me. I did well and was content when I stayed creative and played in life. Everything started to come to me freely. Not only did money continue to come, but so did many opportunities.

At the end of summer, one of my brother's friends told him of a job doing display in a major department store. I applied and got the position. Wow, out of high school and learning how to merchandise and decorate a major fashion institution in Washington DC. It just does not get better than that at seventeen! This new life allowed me the opportunity to live my passion. I did not question why or how it came to me; I just allowed it all to happen. It was a very happy and prosperous time for me.

The idea of going on to college was the furthest thing from my mind. I felt I had finally found my niche in life, and it was a joyous experience. As time went on, my work got better and so did my confidence. I was attracting wonderful people and wonderful experiences in my work and my social life.

New Skills and Challenges

As more confidence and happiness came into my life, so did the unhappy and insecure people. Being young, and conditioned by my parents, I bought into their fear instead of allowing them to be the unhappy, insecure people they were. People who don't love themselves must have a need to accommodate those who are unhappy. It just seems easier to try to make others happy instead of taking the time to see the truth and take responsibility for your own happiness.

I was very good at my job. My peers started to feel threatened by me, and then my boss started getting insecure. People I worked with began to tell me that I needed to do things differently. I realized that I needed to change the way I was seeing things, but again, I became a small boy playing with the other kids. I felt like a useless and disappointing child when I was around my boss. I needed to change the way I was thinking. I was doing it wrong, too much information.... I was starting to doubt myself and things just suddenly were not working for me.

Once again, I was not in a happy space. I knew how to do the job with my talent, but I realized that I was doing my work the way the others wanted me to do it. By doing it their way, I was miserable, scared and felt like giving up. I was giving them power, and losing control. I kept thinking, "Where is the passion?" I know how that felt, I must get it back.

I refused to give it up! I started not to buy into this thought. I knew this was the correct job for me. Things started feeling negative, but I realized that I had changed, not the people I worked with. Though happy with myself, I was around people who were not happy with themselves. As a result I did not feel good anymore. That space where they were must have been where I was at the time that I took that particular job. I was changing, not the people around me.

Funny how we do not see clearly when we are in the midst of growth. Things seem difficult and strange, and we start to believe that we are doing something wrong. In reality, we have not only grown out of the situation, but also with the surroundings.

For now I had become a visual trimmer and a wonderful artist at my craft. I allowed that to be, and knew that something in my environment had to change as well. I loved what I was doing too much. I only surrounded my thoughts with love for what I was doing, and knew that believing in what I was doing and feeling good about it would open something up for me.

My Own Store!

Out of the blue, the executives of the company came to me and offered me my own store to manage. Where did this come from? Wow, my own store at twenty? Things are a-changing now! If I had been more aware at the time, I would have understood that I manifested that store. My good fortune came because I believed in myself and stopped listening to others, and followed my passion. God handed this opportunity to me and gave me the choice to move into that position, away from the negativity that was not bringing me my joy!

Instead my thought at the time was that I was destined to be a great designer! I was aware others had great talent. I did not realize at the time that the Universe was just reacting to my vibration, and giving me what I felt I deserved. The law of attraction was at work, and I was clueless.

I started working in my own store and it was grand. I got to hire people to execute my ideas. Again I was enjoying my life. I was able to get my first apartment and really be who I wanted to be all of my life, without feeling that I was bad or ugly for being that way. Time went by, and I was introduced to my first love.

Falling In Love and Falling Apart

Relating to different kinds of people on a daily basis and still being able to retain happiness was strange. Being intimate with someone on a daily basis was even stranger. I fell head over heels for this person. For the first time in my life I was normal! Young, a great job, and now romance. Who could ask for anything more?

All was grand, and then I was informed that my ex-boss was now getting a promotion. He would be in charge of a group of stores, and since we worked together before so well he was now going to be over me once again. Oh rapture! I started to get knots in my stomach. I would go home and my partner would start telling me how to dress and how I should be acting. Nothing seemed right at work, and now, not in my personal life either.

As soon as I started fearing, I started losing. Just like when I was very young. Oh, to be young and understand these things. Everything started to fall apart. I was lost once again and very unhappy. Not understanding the law of attraction at that time, I did understand that I needed to focus on my passion. I knew myself to be a great designer, and I needed to figure out how to find that place again. I refused to give up my dream. I felt it and believed it.

Out of the blue, I got a call from another divisional, who asked me if I wanted to work for her in her territory. Not really wanting to go, but wanting to get away from the negativity, I took her up on her offer.

I was now in a better place, but still not happy. After a big identity struggle with my partner, I broke that off as well. Now I was free to start thinking once again of my passion. I would focus only on what brought me my joy. I refused to have people telling me what I could and could not do. I was open to all and anything that came my way.

New Fun and Learning

I missed my last store, for I had made many nice friends there. I had met a guy who worked in the shoe department. We became fast friends. On our days off we would always get together. On one of our outings, we decided to shop at an old warehouse in the city. My friend happened to know the owner's son, and introduced me to him. We rummaged through piles of clothing, and were having lots of fun doing so. As we were going through all the old clothes, he asked me what I did for a living. I told him, and he then asked me if I would be interested in designing a store for his father in the Georgetown area of DC. I told him that I would love to meet with his father and discuss the project.

I was not planning on anything more than the opportunity to expand my love of design. I was still focusing on the thought of creating a situation where I could be creative all the time. I did meet with his father, and got the project. I brought in my assistant from my old store to work with me. It was so good to work with someone I loved working with.

After many months of planning and working on this project part time, I was finding that I was enjoying my day job just as much. I was putting out the thoughts now that I would love to find something more challenging, but still was enjoying what I was doing, and finding that once again I was on my path of being joyous with my work.

The new store in Georgetown opened and it was a huge success on the visual and merchandising end. Everyone loved the final results, and I was pleased as well. We had created a shopping experience from another era that was colorful, creative, and very fun.

Back to playing in my work and social space, life once again was going well. Even though now I wanted more challenge in my career, I was happy being creative in my daily life and loving myself for living this way.

The Magic of Fashion

I received an invitation from the Georgetown project to attend a big fashion show taking place in the store. Of course I attended, and it was magical. There was a huge stage built in the center of the store, and all kinds of beautiful flamboyant and avant-garde people were walking around drinking champagne and commenting on how beautiful the store looked.

I was in a total space of happiness. Everyone prepared with excitement to watch this wonderful show, and just then all the lights went out. We were all sitting in the dark, waiting for the lights to come on to complete this fun evening.

I just sat there in the dark thinking how I would love to be a part of this excitement for the rest of my life. This is what my work must be all about. Just then the lights came on and the show was amazing. The music and the looks created out of all these old vintage fashions were fabulous. I was proud and joyous to be a part of all this wonderful creation.

After the show, the owner of the store came to me and asked me what I thought of the show. I know I must have been beaming with joy, and told him I was in love.

He then proceeded to ask me if I would be interested in working full time, maintaining the creative and buying end of the store. Also it would mean more financial rewards for me as well. Oh, golly gee! Of course there was no thought about it, I said yes!

And so began another adventure in my pursuit of happiness through creativity. I wish I had understood at the time that I was vibrating a pure thought, and the Universe reacts to a pure thought more quickly than to a thought that is not pure. It also was the beginning of me manifesting myself as a designer.

I gave notice to the department store and started to doubt whether or not I had made the correct decision. Everyone started telling me that I was making a mistake leaving a place of security for something that would just be a trend. I did some major soul searching and realized that if I was making a mistake, I would just have to deal with that. It was too important to me to continue working in a creative field.

I started the job and really loved it. I was buying accessories to work with the vintage clothing, which updated the looks. I redesigned old clothes and created my own look. I was working with other designers and great dress makers. I got to travel and go to fabulous openings and events. It was so much fun to work now, and the money continued to come.

I was very happy. I would now begin to work with other young artists and have gallery exhibits of our creations. I received calls from other boutiques and specialty stores to construct and execute their windows and interiors. Everyone in Washington DC knew who I was, and wanted to know me. And to think that just 10 years prior, I did not think I would ever have a friend.

My Happiness Wanes

There was no fun life in the 1970's, without drugs, sex and disco! It was a happening time.

By the late 70's, I was just not as happy as I thought I should be. I was starting to get bored with the adventures and the people. I had no privacy, nor fun. People did not want to know who or what I was about. What and where they could go, or what they could get from me was another story. I now seemed in demand, and yet I felt very sad and lonely. I just did not know what was missing. I did know that there was a giant hole in my heart – a void in my soul. No matter how I tried to explain it, no one got it, or got me. Was it that I started to draw people who were following their dreams, and instead of staying on my path, started looking for happiness through them? Was I now looking for happiness through a group of people who were fun to play with instead of fun to live with? I just did not know.

What I did know was that I was just very unhappy, and felt lost once again. Instead of believing in myself and seeing that I was growing in a new direction, like with my parents, I was giving all of these people around me the power. I needed to find a new place where no one knew me. New York was too close to home. Where could I go where no one would know me? Where all they would want and appreciate was me – for my talent?

Then it hit me, I will go to Disneyland! Yes, Los Angeles would be the best place to be. I will go to Hollywood and live a great life as a designer and an artist. So once again I gave notice, and once again everyone said why would I give all of this up to start over again? I could not explain it; I was again feeling like this was the correct thing to do. Next stop West Hollywood.

Off to Hollywood

I convinced Laura, one of my best friends, to move cross country with me. Laura was older than I, and at that time I thought much more together than myself. She was a registered nurse, and much more responsible than most people my age. Definitely not a jet-setter or a trendy person. We both downsized our life and put everything in a small trailer, pulled by her new little Subaru station wagon. The trip across country started off fun and adventurous. It is a freeing experience to get so far from your family when you are in your twenties. We took our time and enjoyed all of the gifts God had given to us. Laura, being a hippie and believing in the "Gods," became a perfect traveling companion for me.

We gambled in Minot North Dakota, and broke down in Billings, Montana. Who lives in Billings, Montana? It was all new and fun. Finally we arrived in Los Angeles, California. What a beautiful place! Sunshine and flowers everywhere. Paradise!

No matter how hard I tried, I could not get a job. No one wanted a young fashion designer from the East Coast. If you did not work in the film industry, you just did not dress up in Sunny California. Blue jeans and boots were the things to wear. I would tool around town, without a car (duh!), wearing all of my chic outfits to the tune of "Are you an actor, or are you going to a costume party?" This was just not cutting it for me. I refused to not be the great designer artist that I was, so in the meantime, if I was not going to get a job, I could at least get a date.

Well, that experience was worse than not having a job. It is amazing what people think and want from you, even though you do not know them. At that time in Los

Angeles, the questions were: "What car do you drive? What dentist do you go to? Where are your gym and your car wash located? And what about your answering machine?"

My answer was always "I don't, I don't know, I don't have either, and, who needs one of those? All of which was the wrong thing to say. So once again, I was feeling alone and weird about myself. Definitely not able to be creative, and more than ever broke.

Back to the job search. I tried all types of jobs, and got all types of rejections. I even interviewed with Sonny Bono. He was impressed that I wore a jacket to interview for a waiter's position in his new restaurant. Then he laughed at me when he read my resume, and told me that I could come any time after the restaurant opened, but not to work.

I Teach Dance and Dance Teaches Me

I answered an ad for a dance instructor in Beverly Hills. It was for a ballroom dance teacher position. The only thing I had going for me were my love for dance and some off and on classes when I was younger. I thought, "If ever there was a time to believe in myself, this is the time."

So I went and told the head of the Studio that I was an excellent dance teacher, but just did not know this particular curriculum. I was then asked to show them what I could do. They showed me a few steps and with my best foot forward, I believed that I was the greatest ballroom dancer, and began to dance the steps. With applause, I got the job.

This I think was the first time I really understood that I must believe. Not only believe that you can do it, but that you deserve to be who you want to be. Since there were no jobs in my field, I truly wanted to be a dance teacher. So once again I set out to find something creative, and now believing that I could do this, I did it!

I began teaching dance in Beverly Hills, California. What a trip that was. I now started meeting different group of very creative people. The life of a dancer is no different from any other artist's life. Once you experience the creative process, you never get it out of your soul. It is just as addictive as alcohol or pills. Once you have tasted it, you cannot get enough. I loved waking up every morning to get ready to share all the new steps I learned. I loved watching people go from being stiff, to lovingly flowing across the dance floor.

To dance for 14 hours a day was pure joy to me. It was like nothing I had ever experienced. Not to have to worry about anything but mastering the moves, and watching others improving.

Being Italian, I thought that I knew how to be expressive and loving to other people. Wrong again! Once you learn to lead and follow through the body, you understand what communication really is. You have to totally TRUST the person you are dancing with, or it does not work.

One day I was asked by another male dance instructor to allow me to help him demonstrate a lash. That is when you take the leader's hand and fall face down to the floor. At the moment your face just hits above the floor the lead must whip your body around so that you turn and end up on your tail, sliding across the floor. If you don't think that takes trust, just try it!

I realized several things from my experience with ballroom dancing. For one thing, I learned that we can interact and speak to people without talking. Just by using our bodies and trusting our partner, we can be turned, thrown, and placed wherever the other person wants to put us. This was truly a new awareness for me. To be able to communicate without speaking, just by feeling someone else's vibrations.

Another thing I learned was that when you open to trust before you do something, it always works the way it is supposed to. When you do something and do not trust what you are doing, it will not work with ease or flow. This blew me away, and it is something I have never forgotten. I would apply this in everything I did from then on.

I taught for nearly two years, and always enjoyed it. Was it my passion? No. Was it creative? Most definitely.

Now I was truly a dance teacher with Fred Astaire (my favorite dancer) Studios and I loved it. I started to do competitions and showcases to make more money. That was fun, but it just did not seem to be enough. It seemed the harder I worked to make money, the more I felt sort of trapped.

Fashion Calls Me Back

All I could think of was designing clothes and fashion. Instead of competing to make money, I was thinking of ways to design better dance wear and costumes for this festive industry. Designing and fashion were truly in my blood and I missed it.

In my second year of teaching dance, I received a call from my previous boss on the East Coast. He asked if I would be interested in coming back and helping him on a new project. I would help create the same kind of shop as before, but in a different location.

I had always believed that it was not really good to go back and try to repeat anything from your past. It seemed to me that if you move away or forward from something, you should continue the journey. The reason you moved to begin with was because you had grown beyond that episode of your life.

I made this same comment to my ex-employer, and he responded with, "Well, what would you like to do then?" I told him that I was very happy, but all I really wanted to do was to design clothing. It was always in my thoughts, and that if I should move anywhere at this point, it would be to either design, learn more, or to work with other designers.

He came back with an offer that if I could help him get this new location started, he would in return start manufacturing my designs. Well how mind-blowing is that??? I wanted and desired on a daily basis to become a clothing designer. All the time I worked in the dance business, I was visualizing around the clothing. And here, out of the blue, I get a call from someone in my past to design clothing. Well Yeah!

I think back now and realize that when you believe and truly want things to happen, they start to manifest. I was now beginning my new adventures as a clothing designer, and I was very happy. Once again I was giving notice and making plans to move across the country.

~ 3 ~

My East Coast Career Move

I am convinced our movement is a thing of destiny.
Ernest Holmes

It was in December when I returned back to the East Coast. I had to come home a week earlier than planned due to an illness of my mother. It was cold...very cold, and I was most miserable. I was not ready to move back in with my parents at this point of my life, so I moved in with my older brother.

My older brother – whom I loved and admired more than anyone, even though we had not really connected as children. I always thought he was smart and popular. I always envied his ability to have many friends and be so creative. He had just relocated back to the East Coast after living in Rome for the last six years. Prior to me moving back, he informed me that there would be more than enough room for me to live with him. It would be fun to get to know each other and pal around the city once again.

When I arrived back in my old home state, like I said it was very cold, and I was very tired. I moved in with my brother in his one bedroom apartment. It was much smaller than I thought, and we were not ready for what was about to happen.

26

Challenges and Messages

At first, much of my time was spent with my Mother, who was in the hospital, and my Dad, who now was retired. My younger brother was still living at home. After a few days, I went to shop for a new car. I had saved money from the sale of my last car for a down payment. Everything was working great for me, other than being cold all the time. I was able to help with my mother and bought a brand new car, and in a few days I would begin the journey of designing my own clothing line.

A short time later, my belongings arrived from Los Angeles. I had a lot more "stuff" than my brother thought I would have. He was not happy with this at all. I decided to make the best of it and created a bedroom by stacking boxes and making a room within a room. I thought it was pretty clever. I then went onward, and my new adventure began.

Lot's of things had changed within the company since I left two years prior. I was most optimistic about making this new shop a showcase, and moving on to start my designing. After putting in my energy for a while on this little shop, I realized that nothing seemed to be working, especially the location. The location had been secured by the owner's son. It was not a good move on his part.

This was the one son out of all the owner's sons whom I had always liked the least, and I am sure the feeling was mutual. We could never connect. Our vibrations were like water and oil. This, of course, meant that not only did I have to make something out of a mess, but since it was number one son's mess, I had to work directly with him. Still, I made the best of it because I knew that in the future I would have my own clothing line.

There was a light at the end of the tunnel. This

particular shop was located on the University Campus. One morning I was walking in the area to do my daily errands, and I noticed the back of a gentleman. He was most intriguing to me and yet I did not know why. It could have been that he appeared different from all of the other students who were walking around at the time.

I could only see him from the back, and he was wearing a heavy winter coat, his pants tucked into his boots. What was that about? Something was pulling me towards him, and I did not know why. Finally I thought I was nuts and just continued doing what I had to do, when out of nowhere I heard my name being called. I turned, and heard it once again. I looked over at the man in the suede coat, it was him. I looked again and then realized here was a man from Brazil whom I had met in Rome five years ago when visiting my brother.

He happened to be studying English in Maryland, of all places. We had a very interesting, short time together in Rome. I had often thought of him and wondered what had happened to him. Well, there he was. We had a great conversation, and then I never saw him again. It made me realize that when you want to know about someone, or something, and you focus on just that and leave it to the Universe to take care of, you will get your answer in some way or another.

Making Connections

A different scenario: I had fallen madly in love, (again) with someone who wanted me to sail to Sausalito with them. The romantic side of me wanted to do this, and my inner voice said "do not do it." I remember going to a psychic who told me that this person would not be good for me, for death would be in the future within a few years time.

I did keep in touch with that person once or twice after he moved to San Francisco. Each time I saw him he looked more and more frail. We always kept in touch by phone. Then one day, I tried to reach him and the number had been disconnected. I tried everything possible to locate him and I just could not. I then realized why I had not felt good about going to San Francisco and that the psychic had given me the information that validated my feelings. I needed to let it go and allow it to be.

It is very interesting that the psychic also had told me that I would always be around people who would die, more so than most people. That seems to be how it has worked out. So I am grateful for the information that allows me to allow. Now when I do a reading on someone and the Spirits say allow it to be, I pray that they hear the message.

I realized something important after running into my friend from Brazil: that we should always pay attention to what our inner voice tells us. If you really need to know what is going on with certain people, or you need information to help you move forward in life, just ask and then pay attention to what life brings your way. If you need closure of any kind, just ask and allow the time for the Universe to answer.

Tough Times on All Fronts

Time had passed, and I realized that the location for this shop could not have been worse for the type of clothing that we were selling. Business was very, very, very slow.

When I would bring up the possibility of focusing on the manufacturing that was the dream of my heart, the subject for some reason was always dismissed. It became clear I could not start something new until I completed the first project. I started to get regular visits from the person who originally leased the store and his manager from a different location. My store was just in a terrible location, and they had signed a ten year lease! This type of clothing was just the wrong kind of merchandise to be selling to a bunch of students.

Since business was bad, of course he and the other manager insisted that I was the reason this store was not making it. As if this wasn't bad enough, things with my brother started to get a little more uncomfortable. Everything I did started bothering him. My room of boxes seemed to be closing in on me on a daily basis. Whenever I would buy something or do something, I started to feel from my brother that I was not being a nice person. I am sure that he was going through his own stuff at the time; however, it was not making me feel safe at all.

I had managed to start spending a lot of time with an old friend of mine. He was allowing me to vent on him regularly and I was crying on his shoulder more and more. As time went by, the boxes in my brother's house finally came tumbling down. I now needed to find my own place to live. My friend suggested that I move in with him for the time being. I now had a choice of staying with him or sleeping in my car. It was January. What to do? What to do? I of course chose the warmer option.

Everything in my life was starting to change again. I could not figure it out. I had just come back east to design. I did not want to fight with my brother, whom I adored. I did not want to deal with my boss' son whom I just could not stand to be around. What was up with this? I was just not getting it. How could it be that I was in a place I did not want to be, doing the things I did not want to do?

Even though my intentions were to eventually get my own clothing line, I was taking a strange road to get there. Maybe I needed to allow this adventure to unfold by itself, instead of relying on someone else do it for me? I guess I needed to learn that I could do this on my own, by allowing things to happen by themselves.

I was very unhappy; I hated living with my friend and his present roommate. When I expressed this to my friend, he suggested that we get our own place. So the search began. We happened to find an adorable little house to rent in a great neighborhood. Just big enough for two. It was cozy and charming, and I loved it. I was finally feeling very happy as far as my living situation. The thought of looking for another job did cross my mind, but the promise of having my own clothing line kept me where I was.

It is amazing how much more important a home is to some and not to others. I found that it was very important to me. Being happy in my home enabled me to think that designing clothing would still be in my future. So I set up my drawing board and began to place picture upon picture and sketch upon sketch on it. Even though I did not see a future with my present company, I did see me designing.

My Bumpy Road Into Fashion Design

One day I got a call from my dear friend Sallye in Miami, Florida. She called me to tell me that she had met a guy who worked for a design house out of New York City. She had told him about me, and his boss was interested in seeing some of my sketches. Well, there was no thinking about this one. I sketched morning, noon and night until I had at least six beautiful evening gowns created on paper. I sent them out to the company, and within two or three days I got a phone call at work. The owner's son loved my sketches, and wanted to know if I could meet with him and his sister that week in New York. I saw a sick day in my future.

I love New York. I arrived in Manhattan at the end of the week. I went to a showroom on Seventh Avenue. Gosh, gee! I was in heaven. I sat and waited for a good half hour, thinking that this person was extremely rude, especially since she was sitting in an office right across from me with her door open. She finally buzzed her receptionist to escort me to the showroom so that I could look at the present line and give her my thoughts on it. I started going through the racks of evening gowns that the company manufactured, and of course wanted to change each and every one of them.

Finally, her brother from Miami came into the showroom and introduced himself. He was very nicely dressed, very tan and had snow white hair and pearl white teeth. I found him to be very nice, and yet I felt like I was in Las Vegas and not a New York showroom. He then informed me that his mother who owned the business was very old, and that he and his sister had taken over running the company. He also prepared me to be ready to meet his sister.

Just then a tiny, attractive older women came in with very short black hair and a white dress with a huge pearl choker around her neck. She was like an Alexis Carrington wannabe, from the television show, "Dynasty." She too was very tan, and extremely rude.

I did not feel good about this one at all. Never before had I experienced such nastiness and rudeness from any woman. I wondered if perhaps this is how people in fashion really behaved. Finally, she sarcastically asked me if I thought I could design the kind of dresses their customers wanted.

I responded by saying, "I think I could do a great job designing for the company. It's just a matter of being able to think and design for drag queens." I left, of course, thinking I would never work for this company, not now or ever! Of course, I was disappointed, but also relieved that I would not have to put up with such bad behavior from such a person.

Being True to Myself Pays Off

Two days later I received a call from their office in Florida. It was the brother who worked out of the factory in Miami, the nice one. He said he liked very much the way I reacted to his sister, and asked if I would come to Miami for a few days to work on some of the sketches I had given him. He would feature them in an upcoming fashion show in Atlanta. A free trip to see friends with good pay sounded real nice to me. I had vacation time coming, this would be a great opportunity to make up designs and begin a portfolio. I agreed and off I went to Florida.

I did not like Miami. I never liked hot or humid weather, and Miami was both. I went to Hialeah, Florida, which is the Ricky Ricardo sector of Miami. I spent a total of one week there and designed gowns for the company's fall fashion expo. I remember designing maybe five dresses while I was there. The finale was a beautiful satin wedding gown with a hat that was around three feet in diameter, with white doves and yards of wedding tulle.

I returned home the following Sunday, and went back to work on Tuesday. I was on such a high to see my creations actually made up and models wearing them. I received a call from the design house on Wednesday telling me that three out of five of my gowns were giant hits at the show. Everyone wanted to know who designed them. Also they offered me a job with the company, with a good salary as well. I asked him if he knew of any places I could stay in New York until I could find an apartment. He informed me that I would have to live in Miami, and work at the factory in Hialeah.

Several years earlier, I had vacationed in Miami for holiday. Not only was it very hot and humid, but I had gotten sun poisoning and was mosquito-bitten from head to toe. I had gotten my hair done from someone highly recommended and they butchered it. Over all, I had a terrible time, and swore I would never ever return to Florida. For years, if anyone would even say "Would you like to go to Florida?" I would reply, I "will never go to that state again." Of course I declined the offer. I did not want to live in Florida, and I felt so good about my accomplishments, that there was no need to move away at this time.

I had a great home life happening as well. What could be bad? I went to lunch feeling very good about myself.

When I returned, there was a phone message from my present boss asking me to please give him a call as soon as I got back from lunch. Being on a joy high, I called without any hesitation. He asked me how the week went, and I told him it went great, and I was ready to think about starting a clothing line of my own once again. He then asked me if the company had offered me a position, and I replied "yes." He then said to me, "I hope you told him yes." Well my mouth dropped and I was speechless. When I explained to him that I turned the job down, he then said, "If I were you, I would not turn the job down because you are no longer employed."

You could have blown me over with a feather. I did not know what to say. I called my friend at home and he suggested that I take the job in Florida. So, I called and asked if I could still have the job, and then I returned to Florida. It is true what I had always been told – never say never!

Misery in Miami

When you do not want something and make it known, the Universe will gladly give you exactly the thought that you hold on to. I left my happy little home and my best friend and moved to Florida. Because I would have a six-month probation period, I left all of my things in Maryland, just in case things did not work out.

My first day at work started off rather strangely. All the workers were very cold to me. Most of them were Cuban. There were two other guys there, both elderly, American, and creative. I thought that at least they would be nice to me since we had design in common. There was the head designer and the head pattern maker. Norman, the lead designer, had been there for many years. He and Her Highness, the Alexis Carrington want-to-be, got along very well. I was to be the new guy with the new, young ideas. I was to be her brother's concubine.

There was the owner's son and his assistant. The senior pattern maker was assigned to work with me. I would happily flit around the warehouse making sketches and then going through bolts of fabric and trim to create my masterpieces. I noticed that each day got more and more intense with my fellow employees. Norman would be so cold and rude to me. If I asked any questions, he would direct me to speak with my master. Irving, the pattern maker, was now caught in the middle of the coldness between Norman and all of the other cutters and seamstresses.

Each day my things took longer and longer to get produced, and God forbid someone would be nice to me and speak with me during the day. I always ate alone and was starting to feel very unhappy doing the thing I loved the most. When I would have a sample made, the Wicked Witch of the North would always come back with some awful changes...ewe!

Memphis Cotton Carnival and Norman's End

I designed a dress that is totally sin proof and very sexy.

Any size woman could wear this design. Of course, I knew that a plain simple black evening gown would not please the Queen of 7th Avenue, so I made a very clean, but very heavy trim of rhinestones along the front of the dress, extending down the side of the skirt. When I put it on the model, I decided to put a huge black lily covered with crystals in her hair as an accessory.

The dress was shown throughout the show room and clients were placing orders left and right. Of course, Ms Queen of 7th Avenue had to add the lily to the shoulder of the dress, and that's how it was shown. The gown sold so well and so quickly that Lord & Taylor and Bonwit Teller featured it in all their ads in New York. It made Town & Country Magazine, worn by the model from Lancome. It did really well.

A few weeks later, I was assigned to go on my first outing with the company. They sent me to Memphis to design for an event called Cotton Carnival.

I was excited and looked forward to designing new Sweet Sixteen gowns that young girls wear as they are introduced to society. It was an eventful and interesting experience. Of course, I had to spend several days with the two siblings. The only way to describe the experience was that it was a *trip*!

When I returned the following week I was confronted by Norman. "And why were you gone for a whole week?" I replied that I went to design for Cotton Carnival. As soon as I said this, I noticed that Norman got very pale and then his lips turned bright blue. That was a sight that to this day I will never forget. I just watched him clench his fist and walk away. I did not see him the rest of the day.

The following morning, when entering work I found the atmosphere just as cold as Norman was the day before.

There were red ribbons all around my work stations, and on my tools. It reminded me of what Italians do to drive away evil spirits. I asked Irving what was going on. I was getting mean stares from everyone in the factory.

He told me that Norman had gone home the day before and suffered a massive heart attack and died. All the employees had decided that I killed Norman. If not for me, he would not have suffered such a death. All this time, Norman was feeling useless and not wanted anymore in a world that was his passion. Instead of moving forward with his dreams, he was blaming youth as his enemy and not himself.

Miami Fashion Dreams Dashed

Being young and hungry on my quest for fame and fortune, I was blind to see this. I just saw a bitter old man who was threatened by someone younger and more "with it." When I refused to go to his funeral, things only got worse.

My personal vision was nothing less than becoming the next Yves St. Laurent. Each day, more and more nonsense continued at work. I believed that this is what one must have to go through for fame and fortune, instead of seeing that I was repeating patterns I would experience again later in my life.

I realize now that we are responsible for our own joy and our own fate. We need to be compassionate toward people who are feeling disappointment; however, at the same time, we must not feel responsible for their outcome. Every day I would go to work, and each day I would feel emptiness in my soul. Emptiness in my heart. I did not do anything about it, except work hard to be a master designer.

After my probation period was over, I approached my boss and asked him if I should move all my things to Miami or go back up north. He told me to move all my things to Florida, and that all would be well with my job. So that's what I did, even though I did not like living in Miami.

I believed it was alright not to enjoy my job, because I was grateful to have one. More importantly, it was a job that would bring me the dream of my heart down the road. Looking back, it is very interesting how as a race we are conditioned.

I had no sooner moved all my things to Florida, gotten a roommate and a new place to live, when I was summoned by the Queen wannabe. I was told that my work was not good enough for them, and that I no longer had a job. My probation was up, and I was no longer needed. How crazy was that?

There I had been feeling deep inside that this was not working for me, and I did not listen to my inner voice. I continued to believe that this misery was how life should be. The Universe responded to my unhappiness by removing the cause of the pain.

Discovering Who I Really Am

Never let anything cause you to doubt your ability to demonstrate the Truth. Conceive of your word as being the thing.

Ernest Holmes

I was now unemployed and living in a place I hated. Feeling very lost, I called my old roommate and friend I had lived with up North. I told him I was missing him, and asked his thoughts on what I should do. He told me not to worry, that he missed me as well and that he would come visit and would try to help me. He did come to Florida and we had a great visit. I realized that even though nothing lasts forever, the love of friends can heal so many hurts.

I Thrive in the Transfer Business

Still unemployed and once again looking for work, my roommate's father asked me to come and spend some time in his factory to see if I would like to work in the transfer business. Of course, I could not be a great designer in the transfer business. What was he thinking? But he made me an offer that would allow me some income until I would be able to find a job that did work for me.

I started to hang out and began to enjoy the people in the factory as I learned the transfer and ink business.

I started to find a niche for myself on the creative end of the business. I was taking plain transfers and turning them into much more fashionable designs. I created beautiful displays for the trade shows, and began working with the chemists on new ink and fabric techniques. I was traveling and making a name for myself as a designer in this industry. Once again I had found happiness in a new adventure.

Months had passed and I received a message. My former roommate from up north decided it would be good to move down to Miami, and we could again share a space. Of course I was pleased with this. All things were beginning to work for me again. I loved my work, my friends, my home. All was good and comfortable.

I believe that when you love, you receive love back. Now what I was about to learn was that sometimes you think that you need things, and start loving the things that you thought you needed, because it gets comfortable. Then God decides to step in and send to you little messages that let you know you really do not need anything, that maybe you need to be true to yourself, and not think because things are going well, you can settle.

Maybe what is comfortable is not the truth, but just your parents and friends not telling you what you should or should not be doing. Just as being in love with someone does not mean that they will love you back in the same way. I thought that all was well in my world now. I was on my way to having a great career, and a great love.

It is funny how things work out. I thought that my world was ending when I got fired from the couture business. That might have been God's way of helping me, by making the change for me. I would never have left that job if it was up to me. I would have been miserable for a long time, possibly ending up like Norman, a bitter, old, washed-up talent. Unfortunately he was not washed up, nor was he old. He was extremely talented. But he was unhappy.

The Wheel of Life Revolves Again

For the next several months, I thought I had it all down and that my life was planned for me. Little did I realize at the time that there are many paths and many choices to make. I became quite attached to my friend and he wanted it that way. I became quite attached to my job and the owner wanted it that way as well. I just kept going on with blinders thinking that I had my career and now a life-long friend. I was focusing, not on what truly brought me my joy, but what I had always been told would bring me my joy.

You can see where I am going to go with this story. By now, my friend decided that living and being roommates really was not what he wanted to do with his life. So of course he was not happy. I, being the enabler that I have been since childhood, did whatever I thought would make him happy, no longer focusing on what would make me happy.

Though my work was making me happy, my relationship with my friend was not. I worried constantly about how to make things better for him and not myself. It was truly the beginning of disaster and heartache. How could I start on another path that was not healthy for me? What was wrong with me that I could not maintain harmony in my life? Now, when I had a little time to do things for myself, I was not happy.

This relationship ended, and not on a nice note. He decided to move out, and I suddenly was not his best friend. Most of the time I was not even his friend. Once again, I felt lost and confused. My work was even starting to become affected by my lack of focus and constant pain. What path was I on? Surely, not mine.

A mutual friend of ours had asked me attend his graduation from this program he had attended. It was a self-awareness weekend. I wanted to support him, so I attended the ceremony. It felt very nice to be surrounded by a room full of happy, loving people. Being the spirit that I am, I have always preferred to be surrounded by people who were joyful.

After the graduation, I was approached by the facilitator. He had asked me if I would have any interest in taking the next weekend class that was going to begin the following month. I explained that I had just started a new job, and at this time was not able afford the extra money for such a weekend. I told him that I would be a good candidate for the program in the future. When able to do so; I would contact him and take the next class. He wanted my number and asked if he could call me sometime to talk. I gave him my work number and told him that would be fine. The rest of the evening, I continued enjoying the love.

The Self-Awareness Weekend

The very next day I received a call from him. He was very friendly and used a great sales pitch about the next weekend he was hosting. He then said that he felt such a presence of joy and positive energy from me. He would like very much for me to attend the classes. He continued by saying that he thought I would bring positive energy to the group. He then told me that if I would agree to take the weekend, he would not charge me. "Just come and enjoy the experience," he said.

Well my brother always told me never to refuse a free

cocktail, so I agreed to take the *Experience of Power* weekend.

The event began on a Friday, which was the first evening of an intense weekend. There were twenty young adults present at this gathering. Nineteen guys and one woman. In a hotel room, I started to observe this group of people, sitting on the floor in a large circle. Everyone seemed pretty nice, and this had the potential to be a happy learning experience. The two or three hours that first day seemed to go well and I found it to be very enlightening.

The second day, however, did not turn out to be pleasant at all. Each of these good-looking, healthy people was not that healthy at all. Individually they told their stories, and each person's story was filled with major heartache and pain. They each had these traumatic childhoods and heart wrenching stories to tell about their up-bringing.

Boy I thought that I had a rough start! The only trauma that was stuck in my mind about my upbringing was just trying to be understood.

One of nine children, my father had no education growing up. He always had only horror stories about his abusive childhood. My mother grew up in a large family of thirteen; a modest and extremely proud family from South Philadelphia. Both of her parents were Italian immigrants. She only had a high school diploma. At 14 she developed Rheumatic fever, which affected her health for the rest of her life.

I do not know if it was because my parents were not very educated, or the fact that they were raised European, but they tended to listen and believe in everyone else's way of doing things instead of what would make them happy. This included being sent to sadistic doctors and dealing with Catholicism; having aunts that are literally insane;

living with red ribbons and red bags of salt to ward off the evil spirits. When we were punished, the beatings were physically damaging.

I had no friends growing up, with the exception of maybe one or two in high school. Other than that I had it pretty good, I thought. Despite all the family nonsense, for some reason I did feel loved. I just always knew that no matter how crazy things seemed, my parents did the best they could. I was lucky, I guess, I always saw and felt the good in them, and knew that as crazy as they could be, they too were unhappy with their choices. So I just figured they were doing the best they could.

The Spotlight Turns to Me

For the next six hours I had nothing to contribute to the circle. I participated in all the activities, but had nothing much to share. Finally, after many hours of being asked what was bothering me, I still had nothing to say. Any problems I had in my ex-relationship, or my last job, just did not seem important to me. I was in amazement of how intense everyone's childhood was, and felt blessed. My heart was hurting for my group.

Suddenly, I was proud of all my accomplishments and experiences. My life seemed very colorful and interesting. It was like I had taken responsibility for my own actions in the past and had nothing to regret and everything to look forward to. You might say I felt complete with myself, for the first time in my life.

Wouldn't you know, just as I came to this revelation, the facilitator, Bob, decided that it was now the time I had to learn things about myself that I had never known before! I had just gone through a day of heart-wrenching agony, hearing these tragic stories, feeling all this pain for these young people. Finally I was feeling good about myself, and now the spotlight is on me?

He began by stating how one should be honest with oneself, and how important it was to be honest about your sexuality. Then he said how important it was to present your sexuality in a positive manner. That it did not matter if you were a gay or a straight male, you must act and dress like a man. How men should be represented by designers such as Ralph Lauren. And then he pointed his finger at me and said, "You don't have to dress like him just to call attention to yourself."

Well you could have stabbed me with a knife, and turned it very slowly. He proceeded to remark that people such as myself only dress the way I did for attention, because they need to be noticed to feel loved. That people such as myself are the reason why so many people are so unhappy, and not accepted in society.

I felt so beaten at that moment. I recalled, when I first moved to Los Angeles, how a friend of mine said I would never make it in fashion in Los Angeles unless I dressed in smart clothing, such as Brooks Brothers. Brooks Brothers! I would have come back from the grave and haunted my own mother if she even buried me in an outfit from Brooks Brothers! And I would have paid someone to kill me if I had to wear something from Ralph Lauren.

The rest of the evening was a repeat of my childhood all over. Be something you are not, and if you be what I want you to be, everything will be good. If you don't conform, you will be unhappy for the rest of your life.

The evening was over around midnight, and I cannot remember if I took a hotel room that night or went back home. All I know is I had a lot to think about. When I finally put my head on the pillow, I began to think about all that had taken place that day and evening. I knew that I still had seven hours the next day to deal with or I could just not show up at all. I never wanted to be considered a quitter. So I decided to go back and take a look at what I did get out of the day, instead of what I was told I should have gotten out of it.

I Decide to Be Who I Am

Looking back, I am extremely proud of myself that I did not at any time feel that I was wrong in my feelings, or that the facilitator might be right. What my intuition told me was if there was healing needed from my past, I would be able to take care of things as they came up. If it took the next twenty years to do so, I would do it.

I realized that after hearing everyone's problems, mine did not seem to matter. I wanted to live in the now, and not keep bringing up what really did not matter at this time. What I had learned about relationships as a young child just did not work for me in the present. When dealing with all relationships, instead of giving my parents power and thinking I am doing things wrong, I can just forgive them. I can try dealing with them the way that feels right, until I get it right.

As I thought back on my childhood, I thanked my parents for the good things they had given me, and how fortunate I was to honestly say that I knew what love felt like in my life. And all of these thoughts started making me feel good.

When I was told by Bob that I was insecure, and how I needed attention from people to feel complete, my stomach felt bad and I felt ugly hearing this. I was searching for the truth, and that just did not resonate correctly. Just then I thought that maybe he was the one insecure with his sexuality, and maybe he was the one who had to dress like a preppy guy to prove his masculinity; that he could not dress creatively because he might be fearing expressing his feminine energy.

I then felt good inside. Not because I could justify to myself why I was the way I was, but because when I understood this logic, my stomach physically felt good. I felt joy in my thoughts again.

I also realized that God wants us to be who we need to be, and on the path that we choose. When we are on that path, everything works for us. As soon as we become or do what someone else would like us to do, it just does not work, and it does not feel right. You can be on the path you choose, doing it the way someone else would want you to do it, and that may not work either. Do it the way that works for you. If it does not work, it must not be what you need to be doing.

I also realized that I had much more insight to others than I gave myself credit for. I found that when I used this gift of insight and trusted it, I became happier, and could not only help myself, but was able to help others as well. When you smile about something, someone else will smile too. It is one of life's laws, the law of attraction.

Sunday morning came and I awoke with a feeling of much achievement and joy. My thoughts had turned into thoughts of accomplishment instead of insecurity. I was looking forward to now spending the day with a group of people who could use my positive energy, and a new perspective of the facilitator. I would now see the weekend as a business for Bob.

When I saw that people in the group were feeling as I did the day before, I could now remind them that they were perfect beings. That they should find the good in what they are discovering about themselves. I also reminded them that they had just paid for guidance and information. Like the Catholic Church, and other churches, this was a business. It was a good business, because it was able to touch so many people's lives in different ways. Regardless, there would never be an ending because there had to be a reason for one to want to return, and keep returning. Just like an open question, it just gives you enough help or information so you will return.

My optimism through the day did not sit quite right with Bob, maybe because I was not willing to allow him to control me as my family always had. I, on the other hand, had a great day and was looking forward to getting together with a few of the guys and one lady when the weekend was over. I also decided that I should learn more about my third eye, and mostly, learn to trust it.

I did return the following week to graduate from the weekend of power. I took back my power, followed my emotions, and trusted my intuition. I made new friends, who to this day remain in my life. I look back on the weekend and realize that it was a great learning experience, and it did give me power.

Messages that Change My Life

With this new knowledge and curiosity about my third eye, I started to read books on meditation and learned more about chakras. I loved learning about feminine and masculine energy, yin and yang. I marveled at how each of our energy centers in the body are extensions of our bodies. I loved the whole spirit process, and what one is able to achieve when incorporating it into our daily lives.

In time, I learned to surrender and allow other energies to assist me with information. I found that by allowing, all things manifest. I had allowed myself to be the best designer I could be, and I was suddenly traveling all over the country and through Europe inspiring and performing with my designs and my work. Things were going very well. After a while, I just found that I wanted more. I no longer want to settle, I wanted more.

I had gotten over difficult romances, doubts about what I could achieve, insecurities of my worth in life, and now wanted new adventures. I realized that Florida was where I did not want to be, so why did I continue living there? What I did realize living there was that I can manifest where I did want to live.

I had a friend in Maryland, who told me about a woman in New Jersey. This woman told the future, and was quite good at it. I decided that I would like to have a reading by someone who did not know me, and could tell me things that would come true later in my life. I arranged an appointment with Betty. Betty was a lovely elderly woman who read regular playing cards.

After a business trip to New York, I met with my friends in New Jersey. We drove down to meet with Betty, somewhere near The Oranges. There, in a little suburban home, we met Betty, her husband, and son. I entered and sat at the kitchen table while her husband and son watched TV in the other room.

I found that the information she gave me was quite interesting and really hit home. She started telling me about my three bosses as well as about my disinterest in living in Florida. She also suggested that instead of moving to New York, I would be happier moving to New Jersey so I would be able to keep my car in a safe place while I traveled. What a good solution for me! I could live across from Manhattan and still keep my car.

I never would have thought of this, and yet it definitely was an answer to my prayers. I learned much more from Betty, and saw her several times after that. She gave me many things to think about and many ways to help me manifest the things I wanted. She seemed to always give me another perspective on how to see the things going on in my life.

Once again, I was ready now for my next adventure. I often wonder what ever happened to Betty. When I ask other people who experienced a reading with her, no one knows. I do know that I asked for clarity and she was sent to me to give direction. When we ask for something with a pure vibration, God will provide many people and many opportunities to get the information we need. What we do with that information is up to us.

Expanding My Abilities in New Jersey

Moving to New Jersey was an experience in itself, and a whole new way of life. Baltimore is John Waters and the "Hon" capital of the world. Jersey is the "Babe" capital of the world. Yes, now I would need to get used to many women and many men calling me "Babe." Yo Babe, Wha Babe. Yeah Babe. At first I thought everyone loved me, and boy I loved that. Then I realized it was a cultural thing. I learned quickly to love that as well. It sure was weird though for a guy to be called "Babe" all the time.

I moved to New Jersey with a dear friend of many years. She had lived in New York years earlier, and had introduced me to many of her friends. I loved meeting all of the characters and fun people of New York.

One of her friends was a lovely little Jewish girl from Brooklyn, Norma. Norma would meet us in the city every now and then for dinner and drinks. For many years, I had known Norma as an accountant in the film business. New York was becoming my new playground. I continued to work there, and still travel all over.

When I was in town, I would continue to visit with Betty. The more I was around Betty, the more I wanted to understand how she got information. Betty used her intuition when she read ordinary playing cards, and doing so she helped many people. I knew when I used my intuition, I could see beyond the surface with people, but just how did it work?

Not knowing how one goes about things like this, I wanted to see how far I could take this information for myself. I just felt that as long as I kept the door open to the thought, something would come of it. After all, who would have believed that I would be a designer and consultant? By myself, I tried to learn to read by using Tarot cards, but I just did not feel it. I could read the book, but I just did not buy it. And yet, I always got much from Betty and an ordinary deck of cards. It became frustrating, and so I decided to just to leave it alone.

One evening Norma called to speak to my roommate. My roommate was on location working at the time, so Norma and I chatted. She was looking for a book that she had lent to my roommate, *We Don't Die*, which is George Anderson's conversations with the other side. I could not believe that Norma had been the one that turned my roommate on to that book! I had read the book and loved it. My curiosity led me to question how she felt about the book and about life on the other side. After a long conversation, I learned that she was more than just an accountant, she also was extremely psychic, and was studying massage therapy. In her sixties, she decided to give up working in film and wanted to become a message therapist. Wow!

And if that was not enough, she was planning to go to India to study with a Guru. I was amazed and found myself in awe of such a lady. And definitely felt I was exploring another planet. I was actually now talking to someone who was interested in something that I was starting to feel passionate about.

I asked her how I could learn more and where I could study to develop my powers. She then said, "why don't you meet us in the city on Tuesday evenings?"

In Manhattan was a woman named Celeste. She held classes in the basement of an old church, where she taught people to develop their psychic knowledge. Well, of course I was there every Tuesday evening that I was in town. I would meet with Norma and a great group of interesting, but very different people. There I learned about psychic surgery and how to read energy. I loved those classes. The first thing that we did was to hold each other's ring and feel the energy, then with our eyes closed, described what pictures would come into our minds. I learned so much about myself and how to understand others.

Divine Guidance Again

Then my roommate decided to move. She had decided to relocate to Los Angeles. I continued to attend the classes and saw Norma less and less. She had quit the film business and had started her massage business full time. She was quite successful at it, and I heard she was very good. For someone in her sixties and being all of about 4' 11", I heard she had the strength of a man and the touch of the Gods.

Being now in my 30's, I was quite impressed with all of this. I took classes and continued traveling all over the world as a consultant for the textile industry.

After a while I realized that the little closet I lived in

was not where I wanted to call home anymore. I just could not make a decision as to what to do, and where to go next. Each time I returned to my apartment, it no longer felt like home to me. Again, I just left it alone, and waited for a sign or an answer.

On a cold, snowy day I woke up with a terrible tooth ache. I went to a local dentist who told me I needed a root canal, and of course found many other things wrong. There would be about $10,000.00 worth of dental work needed. Wow! That was a bit of news. I went to class the next evening and asked what this meant? Why did I manifest a root canal? They told me that when you have any problems with your gums or teeth, this meant that you needed to start making decisions with your life. And now I had to start making big decisions. I was feeling the need to change, but I was just too lazy to move or do anything about it. I had gotten comfortable in my closet, my new friends, and my classes.

I was speaking to a friend who suggested that I seek out a dental college to take care of my teeth. What a great idea. They would be supervised and charge half of the fee if not less. Here again is another time that God had decided to make the decision for me. My intuition told me it was time to move forward, and I ignored my feelings. I could stay where I was, feeling not at home and pay off the surgery for a while, or make a change, find a new home, and not feel overwhelmed by the surgery.

I saw another adventure brewing. Where is a good dental college? Doing research, I found that it would take a long time to take care of what I needed done. I also found out that the University of Maryland in Baltimore had a great school of Dentistry. Gee... did I want to live that close to my parents?

~ 5 ~

Baltimore and Mom's Journey Home

*I do not believe that God has imposed suffering upon anyone to
punish them or to teach them a lesson.*

Ernest Holmes

I called a friend in Columbia, Maryland to let her
know that I was thinking about moving back to the
DC area. I told her what I was planning on doing, and
was considering the University of Maryland to get my
work done. She asked me if I had considered living in
Baltimore City. I had no clue, I never thought of Baltimore
as an option. I just wanted somewhere I could feel
comfortable living and that was near an airport so that
I could travel easily for work.

"Funny that you should want to be near the University.
We just purchased an old Brownstone in the City."

I could have the second floor flat for a very reasonable
price and still be close enough to both the airport and the
college. Well, the decision was made. My new adventure
was beginning to manifest. I could not make a decision
of where I wanted to be next, so God helped me once
again. The solution came when I started focusing on what
I needed to do for myself, then surrendered to it.

Well, I packed up and started for another adventure
in Baltimore. I gave up my classes in the city. I also lost

touch with Norma. I miss Norma, and often wondered what became of her. God surely gave me an angel in Norma to direct me in my adventures.

"Home" in Baltimore

Baltimore: fun, funky and old. I moved from a place that called me "babe" to a place that called me "Hon." What an adventure this was going to be!

I had a large flat on the second floor of an old brownstone. It was at the end of a street next to a roadway. Across the roadway was the prison. On the other end was an old beautiful hotel. I am not sure, but I think it was called the Belvedere. I turned the flat into a great place to work and to entertain. To get to my parking space I had to go completely around the block and through an alley behind my building. The street I lived on was Chase Street. I found out later that we must listen to the signs we are given before we select things. I lived there for one year. In that year, I continued to do my consulting and design work. I was always looking for someone to have a deeper relationship with, but for me that just did not come easy. I was always busy and always traveling. I was very successful in making friends, but for some reason, always felt lonely. I thought that maybe I was meant to be alone, but that did not seem right either.

I decided to focus on getting my teeth taken care of and try to mend my relationship with my older brother. By this time, we were once again speaking to each other but still keeping our distance. Though I was taking care of my health, I still was not doing anything that brought me joy. I was not studying metaphysics, or learning about myself or my well being at all. I was not working on anything creative for myself other than my work. I stepped away from my path to become "the city boy," full of fun and excitement.

It just was not working for me.

I have come to know through my own experience that if you are not doing what is right for you, the Universe will send you signs. What you vibrate will definitely come back to you.

Rats and Realities

One day my mother needed me to take her to the doctor. By this time she had already had two heart surgeries and five strokes. In her mid sixties, she kept looking for some happiness in her life as well, and was just never able to find it. My mother was such a good old soul with the most beautiful skin, hair, and the best twinkle in her eyes. It is rare to see a twinkle in someone's eyes, but I have always heard from everyone who had ever met her, that she had the most beautiful twinkle in her eyes. Everyone loved my Mother, and I can honestly say that I always loved her as well.

It was a very cold day, late November or early December. As usual, I was running late, so I just got up and ran out the door. My parents at that time lived at least a good hour (in traffic) from Baltimore. I just managed to pick her up in time, and then drove another hour to her doctor's. I was not a pleasant person to be with that day. I really did not want to be running errands, but I wanted to do this for my mother. By the time we headed back to my parents' home, it was around 2:30 in the afternoon, and I still had not eaten anything. By now I just wanted to get home and go back to bed. I did not want to wait around my parents' house and hear them argue over some silly thing.

My mother really wanted me to stay and visit. I sensed that she was lonely. When I told her I just could not do this, I knew that she was disappointed. She said, "I smell a rat here and can't imagine why you have to go right home."

I just insisted to her that I could not stay.

I dropped mom off around 3 p.m. and proceeded to head back to Baltimore. I knew I would be hitting rush hour traffic, and still just wanted to get home, get something to eat and cuddle in front of the TV with the heat on. Of course it started to snow. Not my most favorite thing in rush hour. By the time I parked my car and then ran around the block to my apartment, it was about 5:45p.m.

I ran up two flights of stairs, tired and starving, and walked into my apartment. I walked down the hall to the kitchen and turned on the light. The instant the light came on, a huge black rat flew in front of my face, and dove right behind a cabinet at the other end of the room.

Of course I freaked out and called my landlord. He understood where I was coming from, and said he would call an exterminator right away. While waiting, so many thoughts crossed my mind. A very nice man showed up around an hour later and closed a little hole in the wall where the rat had apparently had come in. The doors in my apartment were very old. There were large spaces between the bottom of the door and the floor. Since my mattress was on the floor I was not able to sleep. I stayed awake all night and imagined all kinds of things. Fortunately, I never saw the rat again.

After a few days thinking about all of this, a voice came through and suggested that I should have been patient with my mother that day and not rushed to get away from her. If I had not been such a "rat" to her, I might have not had one for a visitor. I could have had a nice home cooked meal in a nice warm house. Instead I saw a rat because I was a rat that day. This is what I vibrated, and this is what I got. I could have been more loving and more understanding of my family's feelings.

Now looking back on it, I see the difference between protectiveness for one's time, and being selfish. I had no place to go that night. Bringing my mother some joy would have brought me joy as well.

My older brother's birthday was the end of September. My mother wanted to have all of us together to celebrate. Growing up without much money, my mother – who was a wonderful cook – would always bake each of us our favorite cake on our birthday. Mine was always homemade Italian cream cake. I think my younger brother's was chocolate, and my older brother's was pineapple upside down cake. At least that is what we all thought.

Once on one of his birthdays my mother baked him the pineapple cake. It turned out great and of course my brother had told Mom this. So ever since then, every year, she baked a pineapple upside down cake for him. Years later we found out that he really was not crazy about that kind of cake. It really was not his favorite.

Knowing my brother, he was just grateful for the love and effort given by my mother. Why spoil her joy? For some reason, my mother believed it was his favorite, so that is what he would get. Of course, we had a wonderful dinner and that delicious pineapple upside down cake, and many smiles over it. By this time my mother's memory wasn't what it used to be, so why confuse her more?

The Healing Truth

After dinner, my brother left and I stayed to spend the night. Mom and I had stayed up to watch TV after everyone went to bed. As we were sitting there watching Johnny Carson, my mother started crying. I asked her what was wrong. She replied that she was so unhappy with her life. That she had never gotten anything she really wanted.

She said she felt that no matter how she tried to be happy, she never was. I asked her what she meant. She said that all her life she was scared. She listened to what everyone wanted, and did what everyone wanted her to do. Because of that, she never felt happiness. She would always be the first to listen and to help someone. She gave up the things she loved because she loved to make others happy. She did everything for her husband and her family, and never got any validation for it. She did not feel validated.

This is something she also never got as a child. She felt her entire family never gave her any praise, and neither did her husband or her children. She wanted now to have grandchildren and was angry with her children for not giving that to her. I informed her that I did not think that at that time my siblings were ready to have children. She just kept crying. I asked her, "What would you do with grandchildren at this stage of your life?" She said that she did not know, but her sisters had them, and so she wanted them as well. I just sat back in silence.

I wondered how I should answer this. Please, how do I answer this? Just then a voice or another energy said to me, "Just tell her she is not going to get grandchildren from you." I told her just that. Then the voice said to say, in a loving manner, that she should not even focus on that thought. That she wanted something from her children that they were either not going to be able to give her, or not ready to give her at this time. That she should be focusing on things that were going to make her happy.

Then it hit me that, like my mother, I was raised to be a good kind person, and expected something in return for being that way. I loved people as I was taught to love, conditionally. Here I was learning that it was about *unconditional* love, but I only knew conditional love. And that is exactly what I told her.

Believe me I was stunned at what I said to her. I would never have said something so honest like that to my mother before for fear of hurting her. I think at that moment, she was stunned that I said it. After the shock of what I had said set in, instead of feeling guilty, I felt a sense of relief.

As far back as I can remember, my mother had not been well. When she gave birth to my younger brother, it was just too much for her body to handle. When I speak with my brothers about my mother, they say it was hard for them to deal with her always being ill. I, on the other hand, just thought that was how it was. Being told we needed to put her in the hospital was very routine for us. When she was saying the things that made her so unhappy, I went inside and a voice just said to be honest with her.

Not just my mother, but everyone needs to hear truth. For many years, I tried to color the truth fearing it would upset her. But now it felt very good to be honest with her. At the same time, there was a part of me that was freaking out being so blunt with her. The voice was strong and I trusted that. I then realized that this inner voice, or voices, speaking to me were in fact, other entities. They are always giving information to us that will help us achieve happiness. A sense of peace is always joyful and healthy, and that is what I was feeling.

I then understood that we use our third eye to communicate with the energies around us. This began my journey of communication by the use of looking at things with a different perspective – a perspective of speaking now to vibrations, or talking to Spirits.

That one moment of speaking truth to my mother opened up many new avenues for me. I began to see things differently. Changing my perspective of how I saw things opened up so many more avenues. It began helping me move my life in a new direction.

Letting go of how and what we are taught as children is probably the hardest thing to do. I will probably continue to hold on to unnecessary thoughts and behavior for many years. After that conversation with my mother, I went to bed feeling good.

The next morning, I had a good time visiting with my parents. By afternoon I was heading back to Baltimore, and to my little flat on Chase Street. That evening I worked on new designs for the company that I was employed with. Then I went to sleep.

Letting Mom Go

My older brother had left for a business trip somewhere, I believe it was Jamaica. Shortly after I knew his plane had taken off, I received a phone call from my father. He was very upset and asked me to please come home right away. My mother had aspirated and was rushed to the hospital. I got dressed and went home immediately. My dad was alone and my younger brother was at the hospital with my mother. I never saw my father look quite this frightened before. He too was used to my mother being in and out of the hospital. In fact, we were all always on "stand-by." To me Pop looked upset, but also very lost and very scared.

After about an hour or so, my brother phoned and told us that she had been admitted to Andrews Air Force Hospital. Pop and I went immediately to be with her. When we arrived she was in Intensive Care. She was connected with tubes and wires all over her body. She was on a respirator and could not speak to us. The entire time she was awake and looked so very tired. It broke my heart to see her so helpless. The doctors kept telling her to close her eyes and to get some rest. But her eyes stayed open and you could see she was in much thought. For hours she stayed awake, and for hours we just kept telling her we loved her.

My younger brother took my father home and we took turns keeping watch over our mother. The next day it was the same. She never slept. I asked her if she wanted me to contact certain people. She would nod and answer with her eyes. It was as if I could carry on a conversation with her through our thoughts. There were times I could laugh and times I would cry just by her energy. I knew that if she survived this time, she would definitely have some kind of spiritual experience once again to tell us about.

Mother had been in intensive care so many times, and had so many out of body experiences already. This was not new to her. She had been there, done that! I told her of certain people that I had contacted. I could really feel when she was happy about whom I I told, and I could feel when she was angry about certain people I contacted. When I told her that I called my older brother, I felt he was the one person she was really holding on for. He had just landed on his trip and was checking into his hotel when I called him and told him to return. As I told her that he was on his way back, that beautiful sparkle that was only hers began to radiate. She was very happy.

It was about eight o'clock in the evening when I went in to see her again. We were waiting for my brother to arrive. Mom had been waiting so patiently for him to come. I just stood there watching, she was so tired and so frail. I prayed and asked my Inner Voice, to please give me something to say to her that would help her. Words just started speaking through me. I had not a thought of what I was saying. I said to her "Why are you not sleeping? Are you afraid if you close your eyes you will die? She nodded as if to say yes. I asked her if she was afraid that she would not get to see my brother. She again responded yes. I told her that she needed to sleep, or she would not be aware when my brother did get there. I also promised her that my brother would be there soon and that she should not fear; that God was in the room with her and he would be there to help her. She smiled at me and closed her eyes. I called the nurse in to make sure that she was alright. The nurse said that she was finally sleeping. This would be the best thing for her at this time. I thanked the Voice and with a feeling of peace, went back to the waiting room.

My brother finally got to the hospital around 9:30 in the evening. We went immediately in to see mom. When we got there she was still asleep. We just waited for maybe ten minutes or so, and she then opened her eyes. She was aware and very happy to see her eldest son. I left them, so that they could have some time alone. It was past 11:30, and we decided to let mother get some rest, and also get some rest ourselves. My brother and I went to an old friend's nearby. We arrived there and went right to bed.

Insights in Goodbye

About an hour later the phone rang. It was the hospital informing us that mother had just gone into a state of rest. The machine was now keeping her alive. It was time for us to make a decision.

In the morning my younger brother brought dad to the hospital where we all met with the doctor. He informed us that my mother was gone, and the machines were the only thing keeping her alive. Emotionally zoned, my brothers and I just kind of looked at each other with no idea of how to make a decision. Just then my father came out of a dazed state which he had been in for the past two days and said,

"She would not be happy in a state of *not being*."

At the same moment, we each got our answers, and allowed our beloved mother to move on. Saying goodbye to my mother made me joyously aware that I was helping her go back to a space that she had been preparing to go to for many years. I realized that the conversation we had a few evenings back was her way of saying, "I want to go to a different place now." I think that her body was tired and she was asking for validation to move to another space. She wanted me to hear that there would be no grandchildren at this time for her. She wanted me to understand that she had not been happy in the physical for a long time. She was done in the physical. She was preparing to be with her mother and father who she was missing so much. I believe she was telling me at that evening that she wanted to be a little girl again without a husband, and without feeling she had to do for everyone else. I am sure that she did not care whether or not she saw her siblings or friends, because she did not want to say goodbye and feel guilty for not wanting to continue. I believe she wanted me to understand that she wanted to find her joy her own way. I allowed this moment. I said, "Goodbye. I love you and I will most definitely miss you."

In a few short moments, where did all these thoughts come from? My mind and body were in shock, and yet I had all of this insight. Was this a guide speaking to me? Was this God speaking to me? Or was this proof that God is in all of us, and we can connect to each other when we choose to? Knowing now my mother and my father were probably one of the nicest gifts in my life, I wish I had understood that as I was growing up. I guess they didn't know either. I see how important it is to allow our parents the opportunity to be children and adults as well as they allow us to be. Once we grow we all grow from the same root. The core of life is attached from the energy of one power. Our inner-child remains with us always. Though it was at the end of my mother's life, I feel blessed that I was able to see her as a child of the divine energy instead of just my mommy.

Funeral and Family

My mother died on a Tuesday night. My dad was very weak and extremely lost without his other half. Yes, his other half. Through all the years that they fought and hurt each other, both learned to love each other. No matter how much they complained and were on a different page, they stuck out all of their hard times and difficulties. They learned how to allow each other to just be who they needed to be without leaving.

Desertion is a difficult emotion for adults as well as children. For this reason, my brothers and I decided to have a quick funeral and burial. We contacted her family and began our plans. For many years, my older brother studied much about death and the process of grieving. I learned so much from him during this time. He suggested that we could help my father, family, and friends, by allowing them to have a joyous experience during this time. That this is how we could assist in the grieving process. I was all for this. So my brothers and I went all out in a short time to make everything perfect for our father's and mother's families.

When contacting her family, I found that they were very concerned about the fact that they lived in the Philadelphia area, and we were in the DC area. They said that whatever we wanted to do was fine. All that they wished us to do was on the day of the funeral to have my mother's coffin open in the church, so that the family could view the body for the very last time.

Italian Catholic funerals are such a ritual. The other request was that even though we were in Maryland and they lived near their brothers in Pennsylvania, we would have to make a separate call to my uncle's to let them know their sister had passed. I could understand that they wanted to only make one trip to view the body and then attend the funeral, since they were literally only two hours away. But I did not get the reason why they wanted us to call our uncles. Oh well, whatever it takes to please the family, I guess.

The reason that I bring all of this up, is because this was the start of what would be a very ugly, hurtful day. My aunts did show up, but not when they said they were going to show up. They criticized everything that was done. They wanted us to be rude to people we loved, and they were very rude to my father. They showed me a side of them that I just had never known before. Maybe I had seen it, but I do not want to think that I had experienced it before. It was very petty and shallow. Hurtful and mean.

As I look back on it now I see that maybe this was all about ego and not about love. Maybe this was part of their grieving process. I know I was devastated. I overlooked all the nastiness and even apologized to them for all of the upset that took place, but they did not seem to want to accept my apology. I felt hurt and confused. Here my mother had just passed away, and I was watching my father in much pain. And now the family that I was always told were the most important people in my life were just being very ugly.

I had to go within myself and ask what it was I needed to do now. Should I hold the pain inside and forget it ever happened? Should I agree with them and believe the awful things about people and my father that they wanted me to believe? Should I tell them off and treat them mean as they had treated me and my family? I prayed, and I thought, and I waited to hear a voice.

After many days of feeling much guilt, a voice did come and speak to me. It said "Dino, are you shocked to find out that these people are and always have been this way? If you met them in a club or at a party, would you want to be friends with people who act like this? Do you want to be around people like this?" I thought to myself that my life was too precious to allow this treatment from any one. If I had the option to choose, would I accept this as good behavior from a person? And then the voice said to me, "You do have the choice."

At that point, I realized that this family was important to my mother, not to me. That she bought into their idea of what family and love was all about. It had nothing to do with me. That I did not have to allow them to bully me like they had bullied her. All Mother had really wanted was for them to allow her to be happy with the choices she had made. I came to understand that I could love them for being who they were, but I did not have to have them in my life.

To this day I do love them all; however, when it comes to getting together, I just do not have anything to say to them. So I allow it to be. I have great relationships with other family members that I chose to have in my life. The wonderful teaching of the Spirit is that we all have the ability to choose our own experience. If we want it to be beautiful, it will be just that. If we want to surround ourselves with people who bring us our joy, we can.

This was a very profound time in my life. I learned so much after my mother's death. I had always surrounded myself with people who I thought would bring me joy, instead of being joyous and surrounding myself with joyous people. Wow, I should have had a V-8! From this experience, I am so grateful for the people that I invite into my life, as well as for those who are in my life to teach me.

~ 6 ~

West Coast and Dad's Final Chapter

*Life is mirror and will reflect back to the thinker
what he thinks into it.*

Ernest Holmes

After a while, work opportunities were becoming fewer and fewer. I was now making frequent trips to the west coast to do work with manufacturers there. A recession was hitting the East Coast big time, and people were just not paying for creativity. Many of my West Coast friends were telling me to move back to California where there would never be a recession. So of course another new adventure started to manifest. I gave everyone notice that I was planning on moving back to the West Coast.

New and Old Friends – Life is Good!

Of course, everyone on the East Coast thinks that you are crazy for going to the West Coast, even more so to Los Angeles. I finished a couple of New York business trips. But before my last trip to New York ended, I received a phone call from my older brother. He was visiting Los Angeles on holiday, and fell in love with California, of course. He managed to track me down and asked if I would mind if he came out to LA with me. He already had secured a job and a place to live. I was totally blown away at his immediate decision. I agreed and was very happy that he was coming along, and very happy for him as well. So one week later we packed a truck and headed for the City of Angels.

Once I got there I started booking myself between both coasts to work. I moved in with my dear friend of many years from Florida who was in the film business. It was great being back in Los Angeles. The weather was always wonderful on the west side of town. My brother found a place in West Hollywood. I managed to be very busy my first year in L. A.

Between working and getting reacquainted with old friends and meeting new ones, I think back and life was going pretty well, and I was very happy. About a year and a half went by, and business started to slow down for me once again. The recession decided to hit the town that could never have problems. A friend from back home decided that he did not want to work any longer at his present job. He wanted to relocate to the West Coast with his partner. He had an interest in us working together. I was so very excited to have them both living near me again. I agreed, and we began flying back and forth, making plans and getting things together for our future business.

I had another friend of many years who lived in Los Angeles as well. My father had adored her, and was very happy about me living close to her. She lived with her husband in the Valley. When it came to me, my dad only thought with unconditional love. I know that he was very lost without my mother. He felt abandoned by his and my mother's family. He was very lonely, yet he was happy that I was now living near my dearest friend. He understood being alone and did not want me to experience that feeling.

My father always told me to stay friends with these two

people. They would always be good friends to me, and that I should always be a good friend to them. My dad was right. How did he know this? I never really shared that much with him. Was it a feeling? Or did he hear voices as well?

Do our emotions interpret the vibrations that are speaking to us, and then do our bodies react to that? I always listened to my dad, who had no education. His wisdom came from within, and not from a book. With reference to my two friends, I will always be grateful for his advice. The sun always shone; I had my friends and my family near. I was now preparing to create a business of my own. How neat was that!

Dad Collapses

Then one day, I received a phone call from my younger brother back home. He informed my brother and me that our father had collapsed from two aneurisms of the aorta. With my father in critical condition, we flew immediately to be with him on the East Coast.

I have always been blessed about traveling by air. I recall my first plane ride when I was 16 to Denver, Colorado. The only thing I knew about flying was that my dad and older brother hated riding on an airplane, and always got ill. So when I got invited to go to Denver, I just surrendered to the experience. I allowed the plane to just take me away. No phones, no responsibilities, complete surrender. All there was to do was to go within yourself and look out at all the beauty that belonged to anyone who wanted to see it.

Just being in the clouds and watching the colors is enough to tell you that God exists. This was one plane ride that I was truly grateful for. Under the circumstances, I could have been a basket case, but instead I went within and asked my inner voice to tell me how I should deal with this. It just kept saying for me to allow and all will work out fine.

Pop's condition was pretty bad. He had corrective surgery and was then in Intensive Care for a month. He then went into a regular room for an additional month to heal. My brother returned to Los Angeles after a week or so, and I remained with my younger brother and dad. It was a very hard time for my father. I am sure that his heart was broken since my mother's death, and now two of his son's being 3000 miles away. Isn't it funny how he missed two of his children, and then his body manifested two aneurisms in his heart area? That always stayed in my mind.

After two months in the hospital, we were able to bring Pop home. Now the challenge began. My father loved his little house. He had a beautiful garden and a wonderful grape arbor in the back yard. He was always fixing and planting things since his retirement. All of that had to end. He was no longer able to drive a car, which meant that he now had to rely on the kindness of strangers. This was the difficult part. I loved my father, and believe me, we were very different. And although we were always on different pages, we had more than a father/son bond.

Just prior to my father taking ill, my younger brother had decided to move out of the house and buy his own home in Southern Maryland. He would now be 45 minutes closer to his job. I was happy for him. I knew that he had always been there for both of my parents, and now it was his turn to have a life.

Tough Decisions

It was now time for another one of those family meetings. My older brother and I wanted to stay in Southern California. It was definitely time for our younger brother to be on his own. It was time to figure out a way to get my father settled with the proper care. Now in his late 70's, we all understood it would be hard for him to leave his home, his life, and his memories of my mother. What he wanted was for us to return and have this be our home once again. To this very day, when I think of this time, it reminds me that this could be me some day. It also brought back the memory of Norman, the dress designer I had worked with. Watching him turn blue because he felt so threatened by his age.

Recently, I lost my own home in a break up, and found it to be very difficult. I understand how my dad must have felt, and where he was coming from. It is true what goes around does come around. Living in the physical, at times we can lose touch with the feelings of others. It only takes a moment to ask ourselves, are we making these decisions to make life easier on ourselves? Or are we making decisions that benefit those concerned?

Of course being Italian, my father was hard-headed and stubborn about giving up the house. We understood that he could not maintain himself or the house on his own. My brothers and I decided to find a senior living facility near my younger brother's new home. We found a wonderful facility with food service and nice recreation for him. After much work to get him accepted, we were able to secure him a place.

Lessons on Allowing

My dad's new home was a very new and very nice one bedroom apartment. Immediately I started decorating. I brought in all the pictures and things that I knew my father would want around him. Moving day turned out to be a horror. I knew that my father was a stubborn Italian, but this day was the killer of all days. Nothing pleased him. No matter what I arranged or changed, he hated everything. I felt helpless and so unappreciated. He seemed to reject anything and everything I tried to do for him.

Finally, I was able to complete the move and we settled in for a lovely dinner and a quiet night. I had to go back to Los Angeles after a week or so. We arranged to employ a nurse to clean, care and be with our dad for several hours each day.

My younger brother was able to keep an eye on him on a daily basis, and we thought this was a great plan. Of course, dad hated that. For months I was doing everything in my power to make my father happy. I was flying back and forth every other month. I was on the phone daily with either him or my brother. Nothing made him happy.

I was on my last nerve, when I decided to go within and hear the voices. I prayed and prayed for the voices to speak to me. I begged and wished two or three times a day for them to give me answers. I was receiving nothing, and nothing was changing with my father. It was now almost a year, almost an ulcer, and three nurses later. My brother was not having much success, either. Finally, at the end of my rope, I said that's it! I just refused to deal with it any longer. Once I surrendered to the fact that I could not do another thing for my dad, the voice came in. I heard a message that I will hear for many years to come. "It is not your concern, let go and allow God to take care of it." And so I did. I surrendered totally.

The next day I called my dad to see how he and the "new" nurse were getting along. The phone rang and my father answered. I asked him how he was. With a sound of happiness and calmness in his heart he said "Dino, when are you coming back for a visit?" I was astounded with the tone in his voice. I asked him how the new nurse was doing.

He said he loved her and that he had no time to talk, because he was going down to play cards with his new friends. I was shocked. This was too easy. What was going on here? I waited another two days before I called again. I received the same response, all was well and happy.

The new nurse was wonderful and he was now leaving his front door unlocked so that the ladies in the building could just come in and visit him whenever they wanted to. At that moment, I realized that once I put things where I wanted them to be, then surrendered to it and allowed, I was putting out a vibration of action.

The Universe responded to the vibration, that all is where it needed to be, and took care of the rest. All my worrying and guilt was just interfering with the flow of the process. My wanting to make my father happy was keeping him from finding his own happiness. By trying to make things easier for him, I was actually making things harder for him. It was as if God was challenging me to believe that my father deserved and could create happiness in his life.

For so many years I had heard family members say that my father was not deserving of good happening to him. He grew up believing from his own family that he was not worthy of happiness, and he heard this from my mother's family as well. Of course, deep down I never thought that this was what was true for him. From that time on, I stopped worrying and just began loving my father once again for being who he needed to be.

Looking back on my life experience with my father, I see that I was able to find this place of acceptance in my heart many times. My inner knowing has now affirmed that all I needed to do was to love him and allow him to enjoy being who he really was.

Dad's Journey Home

For the next two years, Pop enjoyed himself and where he lived. He even wanted to move to another place where he could walk out on his little patio to enjoy the birds and the beauty that the Universe had to offer. He really was a gentle soul of beauty and joy, as was my mother. I do understand what attracted them to one another and what kept them together. I would later experience for myself that two people can be connected by a certain energy, and stay together because of that energy. For some, that will be all that matters, for others it will not be enough.

Many months later, we got "the call." Dad was once again in the hospital with respiratory problems. It looked bad. My brother and I caught the first flights we could arrange back to Maryland. It seemed like the longest day in my life, and my father was at least another hour and a half drive from the airport.

We got to my dad's apartment very late and called my younger brother. My dad had waited all day for us to get there. When he was told that we both landed safely at the airport, and were on our way to see him, he looked at my younger brother and gave a loving smile. He then closed his eyes and went on to his next adventure.

When my brother told us this, we just both smiled and knew that all Pop wanted was for us to be there safe and happy. He knew we would take care of things for him because we loved him so much. It brought complete joy and closure for me. My dad was one of those loving, kind, and beautiful souls who just did not always get it right. But Pop, when you did get it right, it was wonderful.

Even though my parents have been gone now from the physical for a long time, I carry them in my heart and my thoughts. I talk to them and I listen to them. I was a part of their journey in the physical, and I am connected to them in the spiritual as well. I feel them with me now more than ever before, and know they will be with me forever. That brings me joy, and that is where I need to be with them.

~ 7 ~

A Brand New Day

Each one of us is an outlet to God and an inlet to God.
Ernest Holmes

A part of my life had ended. I looked forward to beginning a new chapter. I returned with my brother to Los Angeles. I was excited to begin a new business with my dear friend, as well as a whole new life. We began looking for the perfect space to locate our new business.

Years earlier when I first moved back to Los Angeles, a friend of mine took me to an art opening on the west side, by the ocean. The gala was held in an old automobile garage from the 30's. It was wonderful. The exhibit had huge colorful paintings of abstract characters; men and women dressed in loin cloths and angel wings were suspended from the ceiling. I thought, "How wonderful to be able to have a place like this to do business." It had so much character. This was the kind of space that I would want, if I ever had a business.

My partner and I began our search for the perfect place to open a business. We saw many great spaces in the best locations. In the back of my mind, I kept picturing that wonderful space where I had gone to the art showing years before. We looked all over Los Angeles and just could not find the right space. We found a neat place in Old Town Pasadena, but for one reason or another, it just did not happen.

Our final place to check out was the west side by the ocean. We found a storefront that we liked, and once again, we were not able to secure it. Everything began to be too far out of our reach financially. But, for some reason, the real estate agent kept showing us properties in this area. We got a call to see a space a little off the beaten path, but still on the main street. As I was looking at this space, I was thinking I had been there before.

And then I asked, "What was this place originally?"

"It started as a garage from the 30's," the agent said.

And then it hit me. After all the years of thinking about the great art show and the space it was held in, and how perfect that space would be for a business, the very same space was now available to us.

Dreams Come and Dreams Go

Three years later, my partner and I were standing in the middle of it in awe. Yes, it was the one place in that location for which we were able to secure a lease. And so we did.

I began to realize more strongly than ever before that when you feel good about something, visualize, and believe in it, the Universe starts to manifest it for you. You will get it at the right time. For me it was three years later.

It's also important to realize that one must always be prepared to accept the responsibility for all aspects of the new situation you have created. I'm sure I will experience this many more times in my life.

We started our business and all was good. I was to be the creative part of the business and my partner was to do the business end. It was so much fun to be working with my friend and old work partner again. We painted and prepared a wonderful office and show room. I had great work space to create wonderful things.

Months went by, and I was working very hard. I noticed that things started to change between me and my business partner. I was so focused on making my business a successful one. We created a beautiful space. I even agreed with my partner to turn our place into a show room to wholesale some items that would benefit a family member. I regularly traveled out of town to sell our goods, and then returned to make more samples.

I began feeling that I was the only one working. The only money coming in was the little bit of business that I was doing on my own. And the business was too new to think that that was a lot. Money was going out and none was coming in. Things were just not right in the relationship or the business. It seemed that my partner did not want to do the business any longer. My heart fell to the floor. Apparently, he simply had lost interest in owning a business. After much discussion, we chose to end it before we got into future trouble. Once again, another disappointment and another little dream gone.

Instead of seeing the situation and questioning what did I do to create this in my life, I chose to deal with it through my parents' eyes. How could he do this to me? I was still learning at that time that I had to take back power and not give it to someone else. Again, I gave power to my parents instead of taking responsibility for my own loss, and for what I had asked for. I had wanted that space and this type of business, but clearly that was not what my friend really wanted. Though working together was his idea, I should not have expected him to live my dream.

So here began another new adventure. Sad but true, do we really learn from our own messages? Or, do we continue to hear what messages others have for us?

During the short time we had the studio, we allowed a friend of ours to use the space for meetings in the evenings. One of his groups included an energy healer. He would facilitate prayer and healing circles there when he was in the Los Angeles area. I got to know and like the group very much. It was nice being surrounded by people who were searching for a different consciousness.

By the time we closed the business, I had come to know this particular group well. I was having a hard time adjusting to the loss of my failed business, but more so the loss of one of my best friends. At the time I felt so disappointed in him, when eventually I would discover that I was disappointed in myself.

I had blown out a few of my discs in my lower back while working. For some reason now that I was not working, the pain kept getting worse. I had undergone physical therapy for it, but that just did not seem to be working. I started worrying about money big time.

The more I worried and blamed, the worse the pain got. At the time, I did not get that my body was telling me to just stop worrying and stop blaming. I was not able to secure a job, so I joined an agency that placed people in the audience of different talk shows. They paid you five dollars an hour to sit, applaud and smile at the camera. I was always getting booked on a show called "the Other Side." This was a show about psychics and other medium experiences.

On the Road Again

I know now there are no accidents. One day I received a call from the energy healer. He heard that we no longer had the business and offered me a position with him as his assistant. This would require that I travel with him and act as his manager on the road. He also wanted me to move in with him and his two sons in Sedona, Arizona.

I loved living in Los Angeles at the time, and had no intentions of moving away. I thought about it, and was reminded that I had nothing better at this time lined up. I decided that this might be an opportunity for me to learn more of how to work with my own intuitive powers. And it would also give me a reason not to continue thinking negative thoughts about my last gig. We did some compromising, and decided that I would do this for six months and if it was mutually beneficial, I would then consider leaving Los Angeles. So once again I was packing for another new adventure.

I left warm sunny Los Angeles and flew to Sedona, Arizona, where it was cold...very cold. I arrived to Phoenix, and then was picked up by one of his students. Mr. Healer conveniently had me start my new job on the weekend that just happened to be a weekend retreat at his home. I arrived to a house full of young people ranging between 20s to early 30's. This also included his 16 and 20 year old sons.

The house was a beautiful ranch style brick home. It had very little furniture, except for a huge dining table and wall to wall mattresses in every room. I was told to put my belongings in my new employer's bedroom until the weekend was finished. I would have my own room after everyone had left. In the meantime, I was to "bunk with the gang." I was hurried through a vegan meal, and then told to get ready for the big evening. It was a costume party of sorts. Everyone had to come as their alter-ego. Then we were to stand in front of the group and tell a story of who we were and how our costume related to our story. HELLO....

I do not remember what I finally came up with; all

I knew was that the evening seemed never to be ending. Finally, when everyone was ready to call it an evening, I got directed to my mattress. I was sleeping in between at least 10 other mattresses on the floor. And it was freezing. I wondered if I was making the correct decision to take on this task.

That evening while I was shivering, I thought that this was a good time to go within and really ask what I needed to do. The voice answered that this was not what I should be doing. However I needed to complete my agreement and make changes later. I took my three big breaths and that is when I saw Bette Davis walking up the stairs saying, "fasten your seat belts, it's going to be a bumpy ride." And that is how my new adventure began.

The rest of the weekend seemed like it would never end. I felt like I was an old school chaperone, amongst the "children." Even more so, I felt like the chaperone to the chaperone. After everyone went skinny dipping in the river, talked of walking on hot coals (the Healer's specialty), and displayed much college behavior, the last group went off to the airport. It was so quiet and lovely. I only had a 53, 20, and a 16 year old to deal with. (Or should I say a 10, 11, and a 16 year old to contend with.)

More Messages from My Body

Once I figured out that I had to be blunt about not wanting to be Mr. French, the gentleman's gentleman to My Three Sons, I was able to start planning and making reservations for our next six months of travel. Our first stop was Aspen, Colorado. We left cold and arrived in colder, and snow as well. But how beautiful is Aspen? I now could take a trip and not only surround myself with beauty, but allow myself to envelop spirit at the same time. That was something I had never thought to do before.

After working solid for the next three days, we rented a car and continued on to Oklahoma. We had really good talks about how we were going to create a partnership traveling around the country healing people by using our intuition, and of course solving all of the world's problems.

I was never one to like driving, and the fact that I was traveling with someone who loved to drive, well... life was starting to look pretty good.

This one day we had stopped for lunch, and during our conversation a few things were said that just sort of wrenched in my stomach. The healer started speaking about how wonderful he was, and how his work truly healed others, and how fabulous it was that he was helping people. Even though he was speaking the words I wanted to hear, my stomach was turning in a hundred different directions. I thought I must have eaten something bad, and this was just the beginning of something not agreeing with me.

We finally got back into the car and went to fill up the tank with gas. As I was sitting there with my stomach in knots, a feeling of fear started to come over me. Still thinking that I was getting ill from the lunch, I was ignoring the fact that something was trying to get my attention to give me an important message.

As we started pulling away from the gas station, and headed back onto the highway, I started to feel that we were going to have a terrible car accident, and I started to feel very frightened. I have never been in a car accident; I did not understand why I was thinking of such a thing, much less becoming scared of the thought. For the remainder of the trip my stomach would continue to get upset. In fact, every time we got in the car from that time on, I felt scared. I was giving away my power once again to my parents' way of thinking. My body was sending me a message, but I was not listening because I wanted to learn from someone I thought was a true healer. This person was not using his gifts to help others, but to feed his ego.

By the time I figured that I was not ill from food, but from my emotions speaking to me, I was in Birmingham, Alabama. I loved Alabama. The people were very gracious and loving. The more I learned about this wonderful spiritual teacher, the less I was loving what I was doing.

Our last stop would be Atlanta, Georgia. We would take a week break back in Sedona before heading out again. I decided to tell him in Atlanta that I would no longer be traveling with him. Even though his clients loved him and seemed to be getting much from his services, I was feeling empty. I just did not feel that his vibrations were pure, and I did not want to play in his sand box any longer. I started to get messages about the clients around me and would bite my tongue. I did not want to interfere with my boss' work. I realized that this was his dream and not mine. That even though we had the same wants and desires to help and heal, I had to do it my way, not his. There was always this little voice saying I am sure he is doing good for people, but I want to do it differently. Was that voice my ego or truth? I had to figure this one out.

We finally got to Atlanta. The house we stayed in was beautiful and the couple who hosted were beautiful as well. Everything went well during our visit there. We were completely booked as usual, and had several evenings of group sessions.

On the last day of our stay, I went in and gave my farewell speech. I told the Healer that I was not happy traveling from home to home picking up the pieces while my employer chose to act very childish and irresponsible.

He understood and agreed with me, but did not want to hear that I wanted to leave. He kept implying that I had not given it enough time, and that I made things happen for him. So I decided to compromise, as usual, and take a month or two off before giving him my final decision.

As you might imagine, that very evening he had everyone bending spoons by using their mental powers. He managed to go through an entire service of fine flatware. The hostess was so irritated that I had to stay up and try to bend 24 spoons back to their original shape. Gee, you probably already know what my final decision turned out top be. I returned to Los Angeles the following morning.

Creating Myself Again in L.A.

And I could not have been happier. I planned to start looking for a job as soon as possible. I went to many clothing manufactures that I knew, many that I did not know, businesses that I had helped create many years prior, and even some old competitors. I just could not get work. It seemed after many years of working and helping people with and in their businesses, they just did not have time for me. I was very depressed and really started really worrying about money.

Again, my disc started to really bother me. I was starting to get severe pain from my lower back down my leg. The pain would begin when I walked around. The longer I would look for work, the more my back would hurt. The pain became crippling, but I had to work.

I went back to being part of audience participation and earning $5.00 per hour. By this time I was pretty good at it. I was getting booked daily for sitting in an audience, and clapping when I would see the sign flash before me. It was great, because I got to sit all afternoon, and I did not have to be in pain.

After doing this for several months, a friend suggested that I go to a temporary agency. Never would I have thought that I could find a job at a temp agency, but why not? I went to the Starr Agency, located in the valley. I walked in with my resume, and as usual they looked at me and said that I had no experience in the business field. I remember saying to this really nice lady, "I can read and I can spell. I can add one plus one. I am great on the phone, and I can file. Please get me one job, and I promise that I will make you very happy that you did." Where that came from, I have no idea. It just sort of came out my mouth. I walked out of the office thinking I will get a booking! If I can be a clothing designer, I can also be perfect in an office.

The following week I got a call from the agency to assign me for a job. I was asked to go to a small branch of an insurance company in Hollywood. The way the agency presented the instructions to me, I knew that this could possibly be my last chance to get work from them. I got hired to be a receptionist. Not great, but I did not have to be on my feet all day, and I did not have to tell anyone about my disc problem.

It was a small office that was going to close in two months. The office would then be moving to their main office in the valley. Well after the first week, I managed to keep the job. After the second week, my creativity won. I loved the job and the job loved me. The agency was loving me even more. By the time the office was ready to relocate, I was offered a full time job. It was at that point I realized that I had manifested this experience. I believed I could. I allowed it to be, and I trusted that all would be taken care of. And that is exactly what happened.

I decided at that point that I would not accept the job. I knew that I needed to be working in a job that would enable me to be creative.

I went on another job placement and again got offered a full time position. It was still not where I wanted to be, so I did not take it. When that job ended because they needed to fill the position, I waited for the next opportunity. A few days later, I was called to take a job at the Screen Actor's Guild. Since I was and still am a film lover, I was very excited. Then they informed me it was in the mail room. I suddenly started to fear. It was not that I minded working in the mail room, but I thought that because of my back I would not be able to do the job. I was to start the following week.

For three days I was in severe pain and thought that I was going to fail. I decided to pray and go within. I did not ask God to help me, but I did ask God to speak to me and tell me how I should handle this. My intuition told me to just do it and see what happens. Suddenly my back felt better and I was looking forward to my next gig.

This job was to be for two weeks. I loved working at the Guild. For the first time in a long time, I was surrounded by people working in a creative field. I got through two weeks, but it seemed like only two days to me. I visualized working there full time, but it was not easy getting into the union. I was told it would be very hard, almost impossible to get a full time job there.

I decided that since I was living in Los Angeles that all would work out. There was sure to be another job similar to working at the Guild. Each week after that, for some reason I was being called back to work at the Guild. That was good. However, each time I was told it would be impossible to get a full time position there. I really loved working there, and I loved the people as well. Finally, after months of going in and taking a job that would last a week at a time, I thought I would stop taking jobs there so I could at least land a permanent job at another place. As soon as I made this decision I got another call to work for a three to six month filler job at the Guild while someone was out on sick leave. Eventually I was able to join the Guild, and I worked there for four and half years.

I Open Completely to My Gifts

At this time, I truly realized that when you put out to the Universe what you want, what brings you joy, and surrender to it, you get it. There is so much more beyond. By using my intuition, I began a new adventure and a new career. I decided to share my gifts of intuitive information with the people with whom I was working. I started to give readings to people from the Guild. I found that the more I explored, the more information I received. I started to see images and interpret different voices.

I love film, it brings me joy. I love being around people who make people happy. I had wonderful experiences and had much fun meeting new people. My readings started to become a second job for me, and I loved it.

My adventures still continue, and my knowledge of living continues as well. I share this, not because I think my story is a great one, but I do think it is a special one. For that matter, I think everyone's adventures are special. Each of us has a story to tell. We learn from our stories. God does not have a plan for us other than to be happy. He has already given us everything we need. It is up to us to figure out how to take advantage of what He has given. He has the answers, so therefore we have the answers.

If we listen and get to know and understand our bodies, we can understand how to heal our bodies. When we put out a pure vibration of what kind of partner we want, we can manifest that partner. When we find work that brings us joy, money will come in. We create our own reality when we believe that is what we can have.

God gives us blues and greens. Water and fire. Air and land. All comes naturally to us when we stop asking God to help us and just ask to have it, and then surrender knowing that God will take care of it. Focus on allowing it to happen, and stop asking when. Your desire becomes your reality and you get it.

Intuition will guide us. Our stomach tells us if it is right or not. Our heart tells us what we should do. Since God is divine and we are extensions of God, then we must learn to trust ourselves first. We naturally trust that God will be taking care of things because we are taking care of things. When believing that God has a plan, then you must embrace the plan and allow God to be part of the plan.

Wanting to be loved, we must love ourselves first in order to understand and recognize what love is. When fearing life, we will be living in fear. When we love life, we will live in love.

It is all good when we believe good. Just ask and believe that it is taken care of, and it is. I hope that all who read my story understand that we all are divine.

The word is at the center of all creation and is First Cause, the starting point of all you see. The word is in your own mouth, and all you have to do is speak it.

Ernest Holmes

Epilogue

Much has happened to me since my last chapter.

Today I am doing readings full time and occasionally get to do interior decorating for private clients. I have relocated back to the east coast where I have started a Holistic greeting card company:

www.holisticemporium2.com

I share this business with an incredible spirit, photographer and friend, David Jaffa.

I have found peace within myself and my work. I work with all types of people, both in the physical and non physical.

I now channel many spirits and can interpret vibration. It seems to get better all the time. And as it gets easier to do, life gets easier to live.

Hearing other voices has given me a better understanding of living in the physical, and a better understanding of our connection to the Divine.

I am grateful for the opportunity to travel all over the country assisting people in achieving clarity and direction in their physical adventures. I am able to do this by presenting a different perspective to one's life, through vibration as given by the non physical.

I now give readings to groups of many people at one time as well as do readings over the phone. As the messages flourish, so do I as a person.

If I refer to God as a "He" in my story, it is out of habit. After all I was raised Catholic, and God as the Father was instilled in me. But when I feel the presence of God, I feel neither masculine nor feminine energy. It is a feeling of total bliss and truth. It is a feeling of serenity and ultimate joy. It is the perfect balance of all that is and all that is (as a true designer) Fabulous!

I conclude my little story with this message: Follow your own path. Stay focused on what brings you your joy and do not try to find happiness in others' adventures. Get to love and know yourself first, and then surrender everything else to the Divine. Understand that we are all connected to a God that is forever good. Listen to your heart and not your head. If we can stay on that path, we will be where we need to be. All is good and so it is.

Now go and have a good time!

In joy,
  Dino

About Dino Calabrese

Born in Washington D.C., Dino Calabrese is a designer and an artist. As a child, he was intuitively connected to people, as well as a spirit who kept him company throughout his teens and into his early 20's. As a result of a psychic reading, he was introduced to the spirit, who was to have been his brother.

Grateful for this introduction, Dino never felt alone as a result of this presence. Later, he began hearing voices from people he would meet and acknowledged that the voices were giving helpful information. As an artist, he would go within and allow his inner being to speak. He then listened to his inner voice in order for him to create as well as to perform. He found that the more he listened to the truth of what he was hearing, the better his work was. When he applied this to his personal life, he always was able to maintain his path successfully.

As a child, he believed that the voices he heard (other than his conscious thoughts) must be those of Spirits or Guides surrounding him with helpful information. In his thirties, he realized he needed to open more deeply to his awareness of these inner voices in order to continue receiving messages from these guides.

Through the process of this deeper exploration, Dino discovered that he has the ability to hear voices surrounding others as well as himself. For the past twenty five years, Dino has been helping people hear their inner voices, allowing them the understanding of how to continue on their life path with success and joy. He decided to write this book, so that those who read it could be encouraged to explore their own connection with Source.

Log on to Dino's blog for news and
updates to his schedule:
http://blog.dinocalabrese.com

You can email Dino directly for more information
or to book an appointment:
dino@dinocalabrese.com

CPSIA information can be obtained
at www.ICGtesting.com
Printed in the USA
FSOW02n0930170316
18027FS